MARIE MURRAY is Principal Clinical Psychologist and Head of the Psychology Department at St Vincent's Psychiatric Hospital, Dublin and St Joseph's Adolescent and Family Services, Dublin. She is a graduate of University College, Dublin, where she is currently a Senior Tutor. She also lectures at UCD, Dublin City University and the Mater Misericordiae Hospital, Dublin.

COLM KEANE is a Senior Producer with RTÉ Radio 1, where he won a Jacobs' Award and a Glaxo Fellowship for European Science Writers. He is a graduate of Trinity College, Dublin and Georgetown University, Washington DC. Since 1991, he has published eight books, including the bestsellers *The Jobs Crisis, Nervous Breakdown, Death and Dying* and *The Stress File.*

MARIE MURRAY and **COLM KEANE** are co-authors of the bestselling book *The Teenage Years*, published by Mercier Press in 1997.

GH00761224

THE ABC OF BULLYING

THE ABC
OF
BULLYING

MARIE MURRAY

COLM KEANE

Published in association with
RADIO TELEFÍS ÉIREANN

MERCIER PRESS

MERCIER PRESS
PO Box 5, 5 French Church Street, Cork
16 Hume Street, Dublin 2

Trade enquiries to CMD DISTRIBUTION,
55a Spruce Avenue, Stillorgan Industrial Park, Blackrock, Dublin

Published in the US and Canada by the
IRISH AMERICAN BOOK COMPANY
6309 Monarch Park Place, Niwot, Colorado, 80503
Tel: (303) 652 2710, (800) 452-7115
Fax: (303) 652 2689, (800) 401-9705

© Marie Murray & Colm Keane, 1998

ISBN 185635 237 4

10 9 8 7 6 5 4 3 2 1

Printed in Ireland by Colour Books Ltd.

CONTENTS

Acknowledgements

The idea behind this book dates back to autumn 1997, when a decision was made by RTÉ Radio 1 to broadcast a series and compile a book on the topic of bullying. For their part in that decision, thanks are due to Helen Shaw, Director of Radio, and Michael Littleton, Assistant Editor, RTÉ Radio 1.

For their subsequent help, thanks are due to the Board of Management and all the staff at St Vincent's Psychiatric Hospital, Dublin and St Joseph's Adolescent and Family Services, Dublin, especially Dr Jim O'Boyle, Edward Byrne and Tom Houlihan.

Special mention must also be made of Dr Mona O'Moore of The Anti-Bullying Research and Resource Centre, Trinity College, Dublin and Dr Brendan Byrne, along with the numerous international researchers whose studies proved invaluable in compiling this book.

Finally, the authors are indebted to Karen Murray and Aisling Murray for their advice and forbearance. Thanks also to Úna O'Hagan and Seán Keane who supported the project from the beginning.

INTRODUCTION

This book explores the world of bullying and the circumstances that may cause a person to bully, to be bullied or to challenge and address bullying behaviour whenever it arises.

What we are referring to are deliberate, aggressive acts which are intended to cause distress, harm or damage to victims. These acts may be verbal, physical or psychological and can range from slander and innuendo right through to harassment, intimidation or physical attack. They may occur just once or, more commonly, on a number of occasions or in a series of sustained and prolonged assaults.

What distinguishes bullying from ordinary rivalry is that normal conflict occurs amongst equals whereas bullying, by its very nature, depends on inequalities of power.

Indeed, every study, every piece of research and most sociological or psychological analyses of bullying confirm that it is an intentional, conscious and persistent cruelty perpetrated against those who are unable to defend themselves.

From the cradle to the grave we perpetuate these bullying abuses against each other. Nothing is sacred, nobody is safe. The fragile, the vulnerable, the disabled, the able, the innocent or the weak may be victims of this aggression we call bullying.

So great is the problem that 20% of children are afraid to go to school because of bullying. Sexual bullying affects 25% of women and 15% of men in their lifetime. It is estimated that more than 25% of women may be battered at some time in marriage.

Bullying in the workplace causes 86% of victims to take sick-leave and it is associated with 14% of suicides. Ten per cent of the elderly living with a family member may be bullied.

Victims may be young or old, at work or unemployed, successful or struggling, in marriages where there is violent behaviour or, indeed, entering their final years.

The common denominator shared by almost all victims is the enormous hurt and damage, the humiliation, helplessness and despair, not to mention the loss of confidence and self-esteem that are caused by bullying behaviour.

Many factors conspire to allow bullying, including our genetic and biological make-up along with the social structures, power structures and hierarchies that are a feature of modern living.

Most research concludes that bullying is brought about through a combination of biological, psychological and social factors, including the following:

- Genetic disposition. What were the initial attributes with which the child began life? Research shows that these attributes may influence how people react to a child, how the child responds and whether the person subsequently feels accepted or rejected.
- Infant characteristics. Research shows that babies who are premature, ill or cranky are at much greater risk of abuse.
- Position in family. First-born children have been found to be more prone to being bullied.
- Early life experiences. Was there early illness, trauma or separation or were health, vigour and security enjoyed? Research shows that if attachment bonds to parents are disrupted, then children may have subsequent

difficulties forming warm bonds with other people.

- Parenting experiences. Were parents calm and experienced or anxious and intimidating? Being praised and nurtured leads to the development of self-confidence and self-esteem, which provide powerful immunity from bullying.
- Experiences of discipline. Was discipline inconsistent and harsh or was it clear, consistent and gentle? There is overwhelming evidence that those who were coercively controlled and punished may behave in an aggressive, bullying manner towards others.
- Was there any childhood abuse? It is common for those who experience abuse to displace the experience on to the next weaker person. Alternatively, they may move from one victim experience to the next, becoming easy prey for perpetrators of bullying.
- Physical appearance. Is the person attractive or otherwise? Good appearance and self-esteem can protect against bullying.
- Physical stature. Bullies are likely to be larger and stronger in physical stature and victims are likely to be smaller and weaker. This is particularly so during the school years.
- Emotional status. Has the child emotional or behavioural problems? Some studies have found a higher incidence of bullying amongst children who are struggling with these difficulties. Clinical work with children and adolescents confirms this.
- Life events. Have there been recent losses, family illnesses, death, parental separation or life crises? During difficult times children and adults may react by bullying others or, alternatively, by showing depressed and defenceless behaviour they may become victims.

- Educational status. Has the child problems with learning or aspects of learning? Studies show that a higher proportion of both bullies and victims emerge from the remedial classes in school. Adults who are threatened by the ability or qualifications of others in the workplace may also translate their insecurity into bullying behaviour.
- Personal attributes. Has the person good body-language, good facial expression, warmth, ability to make friends and ability to connect with others? Additionally, can the person read and interpret the body-language of others and adjust their posture and words accordingly? People who can do so are much less likely to be bullied.
- Communication skills. Did the person communicate effectively from a young age, join in games, understand rules and judge the mood of other people? Poor communication skills isolate children and put them at greater risk of being bullied.
- Learned behaviour. Was aggression used to defend, to survive or to get what was needed? Was the person a witness to aggression as the primary strategy used at home? Research shows that bullying behaviour is learned. It is modelled on the behaviour of others and it is often rewarded.

Some or all of these factors can combine to produce bullying behaviour with enormous consequences for those who are chosen as victims.

Among those consequences may be the destruction of confidence and self-esteem, feelings of shame and guilt, worthlessness, helplessness, loss of sleep, loss of appetite, substance abuse, panic, nightmares, behavioural problems, depression or even thoughts and acts of suicide.

The tragedy of bullying is that there are few aspects of personal growth and development or of human performance and happiness that escape the clutches of this distressing problem.

The effects may be felt at home, at work, at school, and the consequences can be lifelong, damaging the futures, the hopes and the expectations of even the strongest and most resilient of victims.

It is to the causes and consequences of this tragic and insidious problem and to the prescription of remedies and courses of action that we direct our attention in the following chapters.

BEING BULLIED AT SCHOOL

Being bullied at school is one of children's greatest worries. More than one in five children report fear of going to school because of bullying, and more than one in three primary school children have been bullied at one time or another in their school life.

The international figures for serious and persistent bullying range from 5%–10%, but as many as 38% of children in one survey reported being bullied badly enough or often enough to have been distressed.

At secondary school level, bullying was less frequently reported, with 10% being bullied occasionally and 4% being bullied at least once a week.

Interestingly, an Australian study of school children's attitudes and beliefs about bullying found that while many children abhor the practice, they also believe that bullying pays off by intimidating others and preventing them bullying you.

Research also shows that there are specific school years when a child is either likely to be bullied or left alone. For example, bullying may peak during sixth class in primary school but may diminish during first year of second level education.

The reason for this is that most children, including the bullies, are 'finding their feet' when they enter second level education. Furthermore, there are less younger victims to attack and research shows that victims are rarely selected amongst children older than the bully. Lastly, on entering second level education, the 'big fish' become the 'small fry' and are at the lower end of the bullying hierarchy.

Unfortunately, bullying is likely to resume again in second year and a further peak is likely to be experienced in fifth year. As the final school year approaches, those who are bullied are likely to be left in peace. Sadly, this final stage of quiescence at the end of school life may be of little comfort when so much damage has already been done to the confidence, self-esteem and development of a young person.

THE CAUSES OF BULLYING

The developmental tasks of growing up ensure that some conflict between children is inevitable. Beginning with entry to playschool, children of different shapes, sizes, colour, intellectual ability, language capacity, financial advantage, social skills and common sense are brought together on a daily basis. This is often where bullying begins.

In school, children have to learn how to take their turn in conversation and how to communicate with others, how to share, how to accept disappointment, how to win gracefully and how to lose with dignity. They must also learn how to follow the rules of a game, how to tolerate frustration, delay immediate gratification of their wishes, wait in line, take their turn, respond to praise or to reprimands and they must also learn how to become an accepted member of the group. Those who cannot negotiate these early tasks are more likely to be bullied during their school life.

It is not surprising that bullying occurs when a range of children at different ages and developmental stages, children from different family situations, children trying to establish their identity, children emulating what they see at home, children with differing experiences of being parented and with different intellectual and other abilities are brought together each day in the confined conditions of a

17

classroom. In this way, the school becomes a breeding-ground for bullying.

CLASSIC BULLYING TACTICS

Bullying involves a range of cruelties designed to under-mine, upset, insult, isolate, exclude, intimidate, frighten, physically hurt or emotionally wound the victim.

Clinical reports show that the preferred bullying tactic is name-calling, with the intention being to wound the victim. Name-calling can range from plays and puns on the victim's name to gender insults such as referring to boys as 'girls', 'queers' or 'faggots' and calling girls names such as 'slapper', 'slut' or 'wannabe'.

Derogatory terms such as 'spare', 'nerd', 'waste of space' and 'loser' are still used, although less frequently, and the use of racial insults would appear to be growing as immigration provides an increasing number of targets. As many as 58% of primary school children report being called names. Name-calling and threats would appear to be inflicted on girls more than other bullying tactics, whereas over one-third of boys report that physical hurt is inflicted on them.

Many victims of bullying report that they are subjected to serious physical assault and that their tormentors seem to enjoy inflicting this pain. Overall, research and clinical evidence show that a person who is bullied may expect to experience one or more of the following on a regular basis:

- Attention being drawn to sensitive or embarrassing physical features.
- Being cut or bruised in physical encounters.
- Having school lunches commandeered, so that hunger is caused.
- Having school lunches spat on, drink spat into or both

lunches and drinks stamped on and destroyed.

- Having school belongings temporarily hidden, thereby incurring the anger of teachers.
- Having homework or school work tampered with, including having obscenities written on it.
- Being forced to allow homework to be copied by the bully.
- Being unfairly blamed by the class when a teacher inquires who has offended. For example, bullies may attribute blame for missing objects, vandalism or destruction to their victims.
- Having sexual attractiveness, gender or sexual orientation questioned. Sexual gestures may be made and insults also expressed.
- Ridiculing choice of clothes, quality of clothes, their 'label' or their cost.
- Conversations stopping, people turning their backs or walking away when the victim approaches.
- Having contributions to a conversation laughed at or jeered at.
- Being threatened with physical attack. This could include the gesture of a gun being put to the head or a knife being slit across the throat.
- Notes being circulated around the classroom, which are written with the intent of being personal, insulting and hurtful.
- Having belongings hidden, damaged or destroyed.
- Being forced to bring 'protection' money to school and knowing that, without this, physical punishment or verbal abuse may be inflicted.
- Having to provide crisps, sweets and other items for the bully in return for being left alone.
- Being afraid to use the school's toilet facilities or, alter-

natively, hiding in the toilets or changing-rooms during break-times or during free periods.

- Being afraid to be out of the sight of adults or teachers at school.
- Worrying about being pushed off gymnasium equipment, being maliciously tackled and kicked during football, being injured in a scrum, hit with a hurley or having sports activities used as an opportunity for inflicting physical damage.
- Being followed home from school at an uncomfortable or intimidating distance.
- Being prevented from boarding the bus home from school or being prevented from sitting beside others on the bus.
- Being prevented from leaving the bus, thereby adding an additional, unnecessary walk home.
- Receiving upsetting hoax phone-calls or threatening phone-calls.
- Never knowing when the next abuse will be inflicted or what form it will take.

PLACES THAT FACILITATE BULLYING

There are certain locations that have been identified as perfect sites for bullying. Typically, these are places which are dark, away from the regular school traffic and shielded from the intrusion of adults.

Bullying may also occur in corridors, toilets, locker-rooms and changing-rooms, bicycle sheds, outbuildings and sports-grounds that are out of the view of teachers.

In primary school, the playground is the most likely place to be bullied where the screams and cries of children who are being attacked are drowned out by the sound of playground activities.

One Irish study showed that in primary schools, 74% of bullying takes place in the playground. However, the location in which you are likely to be bullied shifts as you move from primary to secondary school. This study also showed that at second level, 47% of pupils reported that bullying takes place in the classroom.

Ultimately, any location may be chosen by a bully in which a victim may be harassed, insulted, physically threatened or assaulted, taunted or tortured away from the observation of adults who might intervene.

TIMES OF THE DAY THAT FACILITATE BULLYING

Certain times of the day have been identified as conducive to bullying. A limited amount of bullying may take place during academic classes. This may take the form of derisory remarks and glances, sniggering, pointing and aggressive gestures. Other bullying opportunities arise during breaks, periods when a teacher is absent from class, changing for PE or journeying to and from school.

TIMES OF THE YEAR THAT FACILITATE BULLYING

Certain times of the year may be identified as conducive to bullying. These include the following:

- Returning to school after the summer holidays. The new school year allows for comparisons about how holidays were spent, what trips abroad were undertaken and whether work or leisure activities dominated the summer months. A person may be bullied either because they have experienced advantages over the summer months or because they have not engaged in foreign travel, exchange programmes or expensive holiday activities.

- When examination results are released. Bullying is particularly prevalent after examinations such as the Junior Certificate, where those who do well or those who do badly are often more at risk of being bullied. Jealousy, anger, upset or frustration often give rise to bullying. Furthermore, the reaction of parents to examination results may contribute to the manner in which young people deal with success or disappointment and may cause them to displace their feelings on to other pupils at school.
- After Christmas, when differences between presents which children have been provided with may again precipitate the experience of being bullied.
- During and after sports days, when rewards and trophies are provided for physical prowess. Children who are physically weak are more at risk of being bullied than those who are strong and have the means to retaliate if attacked.

DIFFERENCES BETWEEN BOYS AND GIRLS

Research shows that boys are bullied more than girls. Not only are boys bullied more often but they are also subjected more to physical attacks. However, some clinical reports indicate that this trend is changing and that girls are also engaging in physical violence. Additionally, because bullying by girls is more intangible, with less visible wounds and scars, the real incidence of bullying amongst girls might be higher than reported.

Studies suggest the following differences in bullying between boys and girls:

- Boys are twice as likely as girls to be victims of bullying.

- Girls are bullied by both girls and boys, whereas boys tend to be bullied by boys.
- Boys are more likely to be physically attacked, whereas girls are more likely to be emotionally bullied.
- Girls are more likely to suffer from malicious lies, slander or innuendo.
- Girls who are being bullied are unlikely to receive support from other girls who dislike them, even if those girls would not have set out independently to actively bully them.
- Girls are reported to be more willing to intervene and to help a person being bullied than boys, except, as noted above, if they dislike the victim.
- Boys express less upset than girls that bullying takes place. One-third of primary school girls, compared to one-fifth of primary school boys, reported that bullying behaviour upset them, according to an Irish study.
- Girls are less likely than boys to admit to bullying, with the result that girls who are bullied by girls often find it very difficult to prove what is happening.

HOW VICTIMS ARE CHOSEN

No child is guaranteed immunity from being bullied and few children will go through their school life without experiencing some bullying symptoms. A person may be bullied for any reason or for no reason at all. This is part of what makes bullying so difficult to tackle.

A person may be bullied because they are small or because they are tall, because they are attractive or because they are not attractive, because they are serious or because they laugh, because they are silent or because they talk. Bullying can begin because a person wears glasses or braces, or has buck teeth.

Being bullied may begin because a person is clever or struggling, because their work is the best in the class or because it is the worst. It may arise because a person has wealth or is poor, because they speak with a particular accent or because their parents are dead, alive, divorced or living together.

Bullying is essentially a learned behaviour and some children have been taught while others have learned to bully. This is important to remember so that those who are bullied are not blamed for inviting the abuse.

However, whether bullying continues to be perpetrated upon a child or adolescent has also been found to relate to certain characteristics in the child, reactions by the child and, of course, responses by adults, parents and teachers.

The following have been identified as possible contributory factors to being bullied:

- Physical disability, a problem with physical appearance or any physical difference which bullies may target.
- Thinness or the appearance of weakness, particularly amongst boys.
- Poor self-confidence, a problem which is exacerbated once the bullying begins.
- Poor personal hygiene.
- Eating habits that annoy or disgust others.
- Unwillingness to conform to the group or to adopt the group norms.
- Attention-seeking behaviour or antagonising other children by subjecting them to long, boring stories or demanding their interest in an unusual hobby.
- Being socially insensitive, clumsy, making ill-timed jokes and not being able to take proper turns in conversation.

- Being unable to understand and appreciate jokes.
- Being independent, unfriendly or a 'loner'.
- Being shy, retiring or anxious.
- Being a 'swot' or refusing to join in social activity because of homework or study.
- Being intellectually superior, good at school, correcting others or being domineering.
- Having a vocabulary that is complex or inaccessible to others in the same age-group.
- Looking sad, depressed, lonely and making others feel guilty or uncomfortable by appearing to be unhappy.
- Finding it difficult to read facial expressions or experiencing problems respecting the personal space of others.
- Having delayed intellectual development. Research shows that many victims of bullying come from remedial classes.
- Having a tendency to cry or run away when bullied, being easily intimidated and not showing a willingness or ability to retaliate.

CONSEQUENCES OF BEING BULLIED

Being bullied can retard and inhibit growth, destroy trust in others and have far-reaching effects on self-belief and self-confidence.

The consequences of bullying may also be felt in a diverse number of developmental areas such as psychological development, physical competence, academic progress, vocational choice and social confidence.

The negative effects of being bullied may be felt in family relationships. For example, children may feel let down by parents if the disclosure of being bullied at school is not taken seriously or if the child is not believed and the matter not dealt with.

Additionally, parents may feel guilty and helpless that they cannot protect their child. They may feel angry with the child for requiring their intervention and support and think that the child should be able to manage peer relationships without parental intervention.

Schools may also feel unable to help the child who discloses that bullying is occurring. They may be angry with parents who complain about bullying or they may be frustrated by the bullies' parents, who refuse to address the problem.

Additionally, schools may believe that they are the victims of bullying by pupils and parents alike. They may complain that they are stressed by inadequate resources, lack of support or insufficient training and guidance on how to deal with the problem.

In this complex web of distress, frustration and anger, a child who is being bullied, particularly if the bullying is allowed to continue, may experience both short-term and long-term consequences. Among these consequences are the following:

SHORT-TERM CONSEQUENCES OF BEING BULLIED

- Being physically injured, having teeth broken, requiring medical attention.
- Feeling inadequate, losing confidence and lacking self-esteem.
- Losing trust in friends or in their ability to protect and support.
- Experiencing anger towards the perpetrators and living in fear of them.
- Dreading attending school each day.
- Feeling relieved at the end of the school week and during school holidays.

- Losing appetite because of worry.
- Feeling sick, experiencing pains in the stomach and constantly holding back tears.
- Being unable to sleep at night, particularly on Sundays when the school week is about to begin.
- Experiencing nightmares, frequently involving images of helplessness or being unable to escape.
- Stealing money, sweets or food to placate the bully.
- Being afraid to socialise outside of school in case the bullies may also be there.
- Being angry with the school and with teachers for not preventing the bullying.
- Lying to parents and covering up the problem.

LONG-TERM CONSEQUENCES OF BEING BULLIED
- Holding negative ideas about oneself throughout life.
- Avoiding conflict at the expense of being appropriately assertive.
- Achieving less academically or at work.
- Experiencing problems forming loving, heterosexual relationships. One study found that 80% of men who were bullied as children experienced this.
- Experiencing intense pessimism, depression, social anxiety or phobia, loneliness and isolation.
- Manifesting an increased propensity to commit suicide.

BULLYING OF TEACHERS

Teachers are not immune from being bullied by their pupils. The Association of Secondary Teachers in Ireland (ASTI) have identified very serious bullying problems for teachers and a steady increase in teacher' bullying. Indeed, teachers have been identified as one of the groups with the highest incidence of psychological distress.

The Teachers Union of Ireland have also reported that stress is one of the largest factors causing teacher' breakdown. So great is the problem of teacher' stress that a pilot Employee Assistance Scheme was launched in 1998. Additionally, EU money has been allocated to an international pilot project designed to address teacher' stress.

Teachers may be bullied for many reasons. The following are some examples:

- The teacher is young, uncertain, sensitive or anxious to please. Opportunist bullies use these situations for their amusement.
- The teacher is inexperienced in handling a class. As a result, boundaries of acceptable behaviour and sanctions for breaches of discipline may not be properly established.
- The teacher is overly-punitive, harsh or discriminatory in class. This can lead to revolt by one or more students.
- An academic subject is taught at a pace beyond the capability of class members. Adolescents may try to save face by challenging the teacher.
- The class is made up of mixed abilities, with the result that information is understood and absorbed at different rates. This can lead to frustrations being expressed in the form of aggression towards the teacher.
- The problem is inherited from a previous class. As much as two-thirds of teacher bullying arises in this way.
- Parents have a negative attitude towards education, towards the school or towards a particular teacher, with the result that a negative message is conveyed in class by their children.

HOW TEACHERS ARE BULLIED

Bullying of teachers may take some of the following forms:

- Verbal abuse, including derogatory remarks about a teacher's skill.
- Refusal to comply with school rules, especially regarding codes of dress or homework.
- Sniggering, making faces to other pupils, raising eyes, leering, smirking or behaviour that is ridiculing.
- Physical intimidation, including refusing to make way for a teacher when walking along a corridor or entering a classroom.
- Challenging behaviour, designed to provoke class disruption.
- Challenges to authority. Responding to requests by the teacher with phrases such as, 'Make me'.
- Asking embarrassing questions. For example, asking for sexual terms to be explained during class.
- Offensive gestures, made either in front of teachers or about teachers as they walk past.
- Insulting graffiti written on prominent surfaces, lockers, classroom doors, on the school-yard wall or on the school building.
- Nicknames that are malicious. For example, highlighting a physical disability, a physical feature such as baldness, obesity or a stutter or stammer.
- Essays designed to embarrass, provoke or insult.
- Obscenities written or drawn on the covers of notebooks or copybooks.
- Insults written on blackboards.
- Uncomfortable physical closeness or touching. Female teachers have been subjected to sexual touching when walking around desks.

- Being spat at, shouted at or otherwise intimidated.
- Outbursts of temper, flinging chairs, books or other class equipment at the teacher.
- General vandalism. When this is excessive, teachers may blame themselves for not being able to maintain tighter controls.
- Tampering with a teacher's car.
- Use of foul language.

Teachers are particularly vulnerable to bullying because they must attend class each day, are usually alone in the classroom often with large numbers of pupils, and because there are no adult witnesses to bullying behaviour.

A female teacher in an all-male, adolescent class may fear sexual harassment and assault. She may be embarrassed to recount the obscenities to which she has been subjected. She may be afraid that she will be perceived as unable to maintain class control or of being overly-emotional and complaining.

Male teachers may be even more reluctant to disclose the degree to which they are being bullied. This is because of the challenge to their masculinity, the fear of appearing to be weak and unable to control their class and the fear that they may be perceived as complaining and requiring support. Indeed, many male teachers continue to be harassed because they are ashamed to admit that they are being bullied.

CONCLUSION

One might ask why so many people feel inadequate, fearful, unwilling, unskilled, intimidated, ambivalent and helpless when it comes to tackling bullying at school? This is the problem with bullying: we do not know what the problem is, where it arises or how to confront it.

People are uncertain at what level they should confront bullying or the experience of being bullied. They are uncertain whether it is a psychiatric problem, a psychological problem, a medical problem, an educational problem, a legal problem, a social problem or a problem of parenting or school discipline. Without knowing how to define and address the problem, it is understandable why people often behave powerlessly, being uncertain how to react and respond when confronted with children who disclose that they are being bullied.

What renders people so apparently powerless is precisely that confusion on how and with whom to tackle the problem. This is partly due to the subtlety and indefinability of many bullying offences, making them difficult to pinpoint and address. For example, we may ask ourselves, 'What is really wrong with being called names?'

We may delude ourselves that being called names did nobody any harm in the past. We may be tempted to subscribe to the myth that being bullied at school is part of growing up, that it toughens and prepares for life, and that it is safer and best to ignore it and allow young people to resolve their problems amongst themselves.

Being bullied is not like having your windows smashed. The damage is not always apparent and the extent of the problem is difficult to ascertain. There is also the cunning of bullies who rely both on their ability to mask their crimes and on the support of parents who believe that their children would do no wrong.

A further difficulty is that bullying at school is also occurring simultaneously with normal childhood and adolescent developmental stages. Some behaviours that may look like bullying (such as ordinary 'slagging', pushing or shoving) may be part of normal progress towards maturity and not a sign of bullying at all.

Additionally, behaviours such as being less talkative on returning home from school, showing variations in mood, being more sensitive about one's appearance, wanting more money or being hungry are often part of normal adolescence.

It is important, therefore, to acquaint oneself with the difference between normal adolescent behaviours and signs that an adolescent is deeply unhappy, being bullied, depressed or even suicidal. These issues, along with guidlines for action, will now be detailed and examined.

ADVICE FOR PARENTS

Bullying has been identified as one of the greatest worries that parents experience about their children at school. However, while almost one-third of parents think that their children are at risk of being bullied, as few as 4% of parents intervene when it happens. This leaves an estimated 20,000 primary school children in Ireland, who are victims of frequent bullying, substantially alone in coping with the problem.

School bullying has the extraordinary capacity to render parents ambivalent, uncertain, frustrated, incapacitated and even helpless. Normally competent, successful, confident, secure, reasonable adults who are decision-makers and problem-solvers in other contexts, find themselves overwhelmed with doubt about what to do if their child is being bullied.

The ambivalent feelings of parents are understandable. Many parents simply don't know what role they should play. They can't decide whether it is better to rush out and confront the bully and the bully's parents or leave it for a while and hope that the problem will go away.

Parents also wonder if they should call the school and get them to sort out the problem, if they should ask a psychologist for advice, take the child out of school, call a solicitor, inform the police, institute immediate action or ignore the bullying as an inevitable feature of school life.

Other parents secretly wonder if their child might have provoked the bullying. They may fear they will stir up a 'hornet's nest' by complaining. Alternatively, they may wonder if their child is the real bully, covering his tracks by pretending to be a victim.

Studies have shown that over 90% of parents believe that bullying is best worked out between the children themselves. It is unclear whether this apparent unwillingness to intervene is because parents do not know how to tackle bullying or whether it is because they genuinely believe that the problem can be sorted out by their children.

CHILDREN'S EXPECTATIONS OF PARENTS

Children who are victims of bullying express great unhappiness, disappointment and anger if they are not believed, understood or helped by their parents.

Boys are often ashamed to tell their fathers that they are being bullied in case their fathers might think they are 'weak', 'wimpish' or 'cissies'. Some boys have been distressed when told to 'fight back', 'stick up for yourself', 'be a man' or 'don't let them get away with it'.

Many girls also report that their mother's response is to dismiss bullying as just the normal bickering, jealousies or bitching that constitute school life.

With this as a background, it is not surprising that children often feel that their parents are ignorant of how relentless and distressing the experience of bullying can be.

There can be tragic consequences for children and adolescents who are left alone, without adult support, to fight the problem of bullying. It is important, therefore, for parents to know how to establish if bullying is occurring, how to assess the extent of the problem and how to intervene appropriately if the problem exists.

ESTABLISHING THE PROBLEM

When establishing if bullying is taking place, a distinction needs to be drawn between the normal rough and tumble of growing up, the swapping and shifting of friendships and the common insensitivities that occur between adolescents and behaviour which is bullying.

Ultimately, the onus is on adults to observe signs that their children might be bullied. The following guidelines may be helpful:

Establishing that a child is being bullied
- Monitor your child's mood. Is it sad and downcast or excessively active, distractible and uncontrollable?
- Observe changes in play. Young children often act out what is happening to them in their play activities. For example, angry, aggressive play with dolls or toys may be a re-enactment of a bullying experience.
- Determine if the child's behaviour has changed towards younger brothers and sisters. Victims of bullying sometimes bully the next available victim.
- Establish if your child's mood changes between school-time, weekends and school holidays.
- Be aware of clinging behaviour and a greater reluctance to be away from parents or other adults.
- Watch out for a reluctance to attend social activities or birthday parties. Anxious inquiries may also be made as to what other children will be there.
- Watch out for exclusion from social activities, especially not being invited to parties.
- Carefully assess the number of school-days on which the child complains of stomach-ache or vague aches and pains.
- Check if the child has difficulty going to sleep, has nightmares or night-terrors and establish the nature of these.
- Make sure that the child is not crying at night. Sadly, many children who are bullied spend their childhood

crying themselves to sleep.

- Remember that any stuttering or stammering may be a sign of anxiety engendered by being bullied.
- Count how many children call to the door and assess the reaction to these calls.
- Be aware of any refusal to join others for play or any expression of fear of doing so.
- Be observant for cuts and bruises and the explanations for them.
- Look out for too many toys being broken or going missing.
- Be suspicious of unusual requests for money.
- Watch out for requests for extra lunch or signs of excessive hunger or thirst despite having brought a full lunch to school. Many children are forced to hand over their lunch.
- Talk to the child about bullying. Above all, make sure the child knows that you are available to help.

Establishing that an adolescent is being bullied

One of the problems for parents, when trying to establish if a teenager is being bullied, is that many of the signs of being bullied can be confused with the normal signs of growing up. For example, being less talkative at home, showing variations in mood, becoming sensitive about appearance, demanding more money and showing signs of being hungry are often part of normal adolescence.

However, there are many symptoms to look out for, including the following:

- Irritability, excessive withdrawal and seeking to be alone.
- A significant and inexplicable loss of confidence.

- Excessive tearfulness or sensitivity to criticism.
- Changes in mood before and after school and during breaks from school.
- School truancy and a reluctance to go to school.
- Requests to return home at break-time or lunch-time. Adolescents who are happy at school usually enjoy these times.
- Changes in academic ability and a sudden deterioration in achievement or motivation.
- Exceptional concern about physical appearance, requests for more clothes or comments about unattractiveness. Adolescents who are being bullied may be self-critical and may attempt to change themselves or their image.
- A reduction in the number of phone calls, friends calling or invitations to social events.
- A reluctance to take part in previously enjoyed activities.
- Signs of bruising, cuts, sprains, scratches or torn clothes.
- An excessive loss of possessions or damage to belongings.
- Excessive requests for money and disproportionate distress if refused.
- Expressions of anger, temper or irritability while at home.
- Going to a different bus stop, changing the route home or walking home rather than taking the bus.
- Sudden requests to be driven to school, particularly in good weather.
- Signs of depression, including changes in mood, appetite, sleeping pattern, tiredness, neglect of appearance, expressions of sadness, worthlessness or helplessness. Symptoms may also include restless, dangerous, wild and disruptive behaviour masking the depression.

- Excessive cynicism, black mood, wishes to 'end it all' or other implied or overt threats of suicide.

ESTABLISHING THE EXTENT OF THE PROBLEM

It can be difficult to determine when horseplay becomes attack, when teasing becomes treachery, when being left out becomes deliberate ostracisation or when losing friends is part of an exclusion strategy.

However, it is fair to say that all bullying is serious because the experience of being abused, insulted, physically attacked or emotionally threatened is one which children tend to carry with them for a long time.

There are some instances where a child can remain at school while the problem is being resolved with the support and active vigilance of teachers and parents. In other instances, immediate and drastic action may be required. The following questions may be helpful in establishing the extent of the problem:

- Is it an isolated outbreak or incident, or one of a series of attacks?
- Is it temporary or of long and relentless duration?
- Is the bullying mild, intense or a serious assault on the personality and happiness of the child?
- Is your child being bullied by one person or by a gang?
- Is the perpetrator amenable to change or entrenched in a pattern of bullying?
- Is it likely that the parents of the bullies will be cooperative or defensive and hostile?
- Is the bullying taking place in school or at other locations?
- Is the child one of many victims or the class scapegoat?
- Is it affecting studies and academic progress?

- Is it causing school truancy?
- Is the bullying psychological, physical or verbal?
- Is it causing the child to lose trust and confidence in others?
- Is the school aware of the problem and taking it seriously?
- Is the child in physical or psychological danger?
- Is it causing depression?
- Is there a risk of suicide?

IDENTIFYING THE BULLIES

An important step in resolving a child's bullying problem involves identifying the perpetrators. The degree to which the problem can be resolved will often depend on the character and personality of the perpetrators in addition to the willingness of relevant adults to tackle the issue. The following tips may be helpful:

- Establish who the bully is and when the bullying began.
- Establish if the bully is victimising other children. If so, speak to their parents.
- Find out if the bully works alone or with a gang. Establish whether gang members participate through fear of the bully or enjoyment of bullying.
- Gather as much information as possible about each gang member.
- Establish if the bully is reacting to a specific event, such as a death in the family, or if the bully is a disturbed and troubled child.
- Remember that the bully may be new to the neighbourhood or school. Immediate and open discussion with the parents or the school might help.

Having established that bullying is taking place, having determined the extent of the problem and having identified the perpetrator, the next step is to bring the bullying to an end.

Parents of those being bullied, school personnel and parents of the bully should try to resolve the problem in an immediate, amicable and unemotional manner. An aggressive, accusatory or hostile approach to the issue is unlikely to help.

The following steps may be useful:

- Establish the rules of the school. Obtain a written copy and determine which rules have been broken by the bully.
- Inquire about the proper procedures for formally notifying the school and for making a complaint about the bullying behaviour.
- Inform the school principal. Provide the name of the alleged bully or bullies.
- Establish if the school was aware of the problem and what steps had been taken to resolve it.
- Inform the relevant class teachers about the bullying. Establish with them how the bullies will be monitored and what sanctions will be imposed for bullying behaviour.
- Determine the steps to be taken by the school. For example, will the bully be interviewed? Will the parents of the bully be notified? How will your child be kept safe during the investigation process?
- Insist that interviews with your child are conducted in your presence. Victims often become so anxious during the investigations that they renege on their story or are

unable to articulate their experience or distress.

- Establish who your child will report to if a further incident occurs and what immediate action will be taken.
- Establish how long the school's investigation procedures will take and how soon you will be notified. Agree on a short time-frame and suggest that you will call back at the specified time.
- Inform the school board or board of directors, in writing, that the problem has arisen, that the principal and teachers have been informed and that you await the resolution of the problem.
- Consult with the parents' association or parents' representatives about the bullying behaviour. Determine what policy, if any, the parents' committee might have with regard to bullying.
- Notify the parents of the bully and provide them with evidence of the bullying behaviour. Be sympathetic to their upset. However, be firm about the need for an immediate end to the problem.
- If all else fails, you may need to inform the police. If your child is in post-primary school they may assign a Junior Liaison Officer to the case, depending on their assessment of it.
- While bullying is not a formal offence, if a young person has been physically assaulted and remains in danger, charges for assault may be considered. Warnings may also be given prohibiting the bully from approaching the victim in a particular way or in specific locations.
- If necessary, civil proceedings can be instituted on the advice of a solicitor.
- Consider moving you child to another school. If you do so, make it clear in writing to the principal and the board

of management or the board of governors of the school you are leaving why such a move was necessary.

- Ensure that the new school has a strong anti-bullying policy.
- Choose a school that is most compatible with your child's interests and temperament.

HOW YOU CAN HELP

When a child discloses bullying we need to respond with concern, understanding and compassion. It is also important for parents to establish if a child who is being bullied might have contributed in any way to being chosen as a victim.

Research has identified what are called 'provocative victims', who are children with characteristics that can put them at greater risk of being bullied. The following are some steps that a parent can take to stop their child from being picked on in this way:

- Discourage bad habits, such as scratching, cracking knuckles, picking the nose or spitting.
- Ensure that the child has clean hair and teeth and no bad breath.
- Ensure that table manners are not offensive, that food isn't eaten with a full mouth or that food isn't slurped.
- Buy as flattering a pair of glasses as you can afford for your child. Get advice about lenses or treatments that would dispense with the need for glasses.
- Buy your child enough age-appropriate clothes or fashionable 'gear'. Being different in dress can invite derision.
- Restrict the visible display of material goods, thereby preventing jealousy.

- Seek professional help for stammering, stuttering or lisping.
- Attend to any embarrassing blemishes. For example, provide cream for acne.
- Seek medical advice for the overweight child. Consider a health club or fitness regime to increase confidence.
- Consider weightlifting, self-defence or strength and fitness training for boys with weak frames.
- Allow your child to watch age-appropriate television programmes. They will need to discuss these with others.
- Consider educational assessment for a child who is academically delayed. Being slow in class can invite ridicule.
- Ensure that your child learns how to swim, to play tennis, etc. In this way, they can join in with group activities.
- Establish if your child needs training in social skills. This may be necessary if their interactions with others cause friction or antagonism.
- Advise your child not to impose unusual hobbies or interests on others.
- Ensure that your child participates well in conversation, responds to the mood of others and understands jokes. It is not uncommon for children with communication problems to be bullied.

OTHER STEPS TO TAKE

Apart from assessing the above factors, it is important to listen carefully to your child and show great interest if they choose to disclose a bullying problem. The following may be useful:

- Praise the child for disclosing the problem.

43

- Establish the facts, gently and without blaming the child.
- Reassure the child of your love, help and support.
- Promise that you will do everything you can to ensure that it does not happen again.
- Let the child know that it may take some time to sort out but that you will not stop until the bullying is over.
- Advise the child not to react to bullying with physical aggression.
- Provide advice on how to respond appropriately. For example, think out responses if name-calling occurs.
- Encourage your child to practice confident body language. A submissive stance often provokes more bullying.
- Advise the child on locations to avoid at school, such as changing-rooms and locker-rooms.
- Explain why the bullies are bullying and stress that it is not the child's fault.
- Reassure the child that now they have had the courage to tell, the bullying cannot happen again in the same way.
- Make it clear, at frequent intervals over the next few days, that you do not blame the child.
- Use every opportunity to praise the child and boost confidence in the days and weeks ahead.
- Provide some special treats, new toys or new clothes, a day out, something that brings happiness to a child who is unhappy.
- Ensure that a child who has become depressed or unable to cope gets appropriate professional help.
- Above all, do not leave your child in despair. Pursue a solution until it is achieved. Your child expects and needs your help.

THE SCHOOL BULLY

Contrary to popular opinion, the school bully is not always an easily identifiable, intellectually delayed, socially deprived monster who beats up other children. The mythical stereotype of the bullying lout being of obese appearance and oafish or cowardly disposition, venting his inadequacies on others, has also been challenged. Nor is the bully necessarily male. Indeed, the profile of the school bully is far from a single, simple, generic one.

Furthermore, bullies may emerge from a diverse range of genetic, environmental, social, family, intellectual, physical and emotional backgrounds. A school bully may be the victim of another bully who, in turn, expresses his hurt and frustration on the next weaker person. In this way, schools may provide the ideal environment for a complex chain of misery.

BULLY TYPES

Bullies may emerge at any age, at any stage of the school cycle and from any material background. However, they form a number of natural groupings including the following:

The reactive bullies

These are children who have been overwhelmed by a sudden and unexpected event, such as bereavement, parental separation or a family financial disaster. Unable to express their distress elsewhere, the reactive bullies may lash out at others. This is sometimes a cry for help.

The anxious bullies

These bullies suffer from deep-seated insecurity and emotional distress brought on by their life circumstances and experiences. Their self-esteem is usually low but concealed by their attempts to gain status by dominating others.

The sadistic bullies

Young people in this category may show little sympathy for the distress of others and may demonstrate a callous disregard for victims. These bullies often have a history of aggressive behaviour. Their self-esteem is not low and some have been found to enjoy inflicting cruelty on others, enjoying the power and status they feel when doing so. It is unusual to see signs of guilt or remorse in these bullies.

The home-grown bullies

These children emerge from homes in which there are multiple problems. They may have been bullied by other family members, by their parents or by the enforcement of harsh and cruel discipline. Their bullying behaviour is learned and is modelled on aggressive modes of behaviour, and they may see physical attack as the best form of control. It is estimated that as many as 70% of bullies emerge from problematic family backgrounds.

The under-achieving bullies

It is not surprising that children who are struggling academically may try to compensate and to achieve status by bullying.

The bully/victim

Research has identified young people who, having been bullied, in return vent their hurt and anger on the next available victim. Some victims also try to understand what has happened to them by re-enacting bullying with other children.

THE ORIGINS OF BULLYING

What is it that causes some children to be kind, considerate and tolerant while others are cruel, unsympathetic and prejudiced? Is it an inherited trait, a learned behaviour, a conduct disorder, the normal rough and tumble of school life or is it just an inevitable part of growing up? Perhaps it is a manifestation of some social problem, a problem of parenting, inadequate discipline at school, the consequence of media violence or a combination of the complex connections between all of these factors?

Research and clinical experience have suggested some of the following as contributory factors:

Genetic predisposition

One study carried out in 1980, which compared identical and non-identical twins, has suggested that there is a genetic component in the explanation of bullying.

For example, genetically determined physical characteristics, including unattractiveness or poor intellectual and learning potential, may be contributory factors in the development of bullying behaviour.

Other studies have identified physical disabilities in many bullies, including unusual voice patterns, clumsiness, awkwardness, poor coordination, hyperactivity and poor control of impulses.

The role of gender

Studies show that girls are conditioned to be less aggressive than boys. Therefore, it is not surprising that more boys than girls become school bullies.

The manner in which they bully also differs, with boys showing greater aggression and a greater tendency to inflict physical hurt. In contrast, girls cause their victims a greater amount of emotional distress.

Additionally, boys are more likely to receive support for being bullies. Interestingly, one Australian study found that 10% of boys reported that their fathers supported their behaviour.

Parenting styles and early life experiences
The early experiences of children help determine their subsequent development. The warmth of parenting, the degree of maternal affection, whether or not a baby was attended to or left to cry, or the degree to which emotional needs were met are all important.

Furthermore, whether there was approval, acceptance, affection, coercion, overindulgence, lack of boundaries or lack of guidance will help determine whether or not a child is likely to become a bully.

Family discipline
A higher proportion of bullies come from homes where discipline is physical, excessively harsh or punitive. Clearly, the parent who slaps a child helps establish the principle that 'might is right' and that the larger you are the more powerful you are.

Research also shows that young children who are actively discouraged when they display aggressive behaviour are less likely to continue this kind of play. The indications are that early, clear, kind, firm and consistent messages that aggressive behaviour is not acceptable will influence a child against aggressive or bullying behaviour.

Physical status

Many bullies have been found to be physically more developed, particularly at primary school, and their large size contributes to their capacity to pick on smaller and physically weaker children.

Social values

Young people are influenced by the values and beliefs of the society in which they are reared, especially regarding the dignity and the rights of the individual. A society characterised by lack of empathy, or that endorses violence as a means to secure wants regardless of the rights of victims, will encourage bullying behaviour.

Studies also suggest a greater degree of bullying, conduct disorders and aggression amongst children in areas that suffer political unrest.

Role models

Whether or not children become bullies may also depend on the models of behaviour which young people choose to emulate. Role models who are successful at bullying others, or who are rewarded for their bullying, may be copied by children. These role models include parents and those who live in the surrounding community.

Cultural influences

Cultural influences include films, computer games, comics, magazines and books. Studies over the past thirty years have shown that the manner in which aggression is glorified, rewarded or punished on television and film will affect the thinking and behaviour of young viewers.

In one study, an increase in bullying in Norway was directly attributed to the introduction of satellite television and to the aggression portrayed in the films which were broadcast.

Criticism has also been expressed about the many computer games that require children to physically attack, overpower or annihilate the 'enemy'.

School size and class size

Interestingly, recent Irish studies found that the larger the school the lower the rates of bullying. These studies found that class size was not a factor in primary school. However, in second level schools the smaller classes had higher rates of bullying.

Studies have also found that 'streaming' (assigning children to classes according to their academic ability) can aggravate bullying. Too great an emphasis on academic success, with disregard for other non-academic achievements, can have a similar effect.

Lastly, schools and classes are organised and structured by school principals, teachers, boards of management and non-teaching staff. Schools are also influenced by the levels of advantage or disadvantage of the communities in which they are based. These factors will further influence whether or not a child practices bullying behaviour.

The school code

The extent to which a school promotes values such as kindness, altruism, tolerance, assertiveness, dominance or competitiveness is very important.

A school with a formal, written, publicly displayed and actively enforced bullying policy, where parents and pupils are agreed on behaviours, processes, procedures and sanctions for bullies, is likely to discourage the bully.

The background of teachers

Teachers bring with them their life experiences, their experiences of family and of school, whether they were bullied at school and their current views of young people.

The manner in which authority and power are used in the classroom will also influence pupils, as will the degree to which a teacher is aware of, tolerates or actively confronts, challenges and controls bullying behaviour.

OTHER CAUSES OF BULLYING

In addition to the attributes, circumstances and life experiences that contribute to the formation of the school bully, research conducted primarily in the past two decades provides insights to the personal, family, social, intellectual, academic and psychological profile of bullies and the people surrounding them.

The following is a summary of the key findings to emerge from international research, which includes extensive Scandinavian and Irish research, in addition to studies carried out in Japan, USA, Britain, Finland, Australia and Scotland:

- Many bullies test intellectually below average or average. It is also uncommon for a child of high intellectual ability to be a bully.
- More bullies than non-bullies have been found to have behavioural problems. One study of Dublin children concluded that bullies were 'unhappy, troubled children'.
- A substantial number of bullies are victims of bullying. Some studies have shown that almost one in five children who are bullied go on to bully other children.
- Children with communication disorders, many of

51

whom are unable to understand facial expressions, read body-language or are emotionally insensitive to atmosphere and to the moods of others, may bully in an inadvertently callous manner.

- Adolescent boys who bully watch more television and videos with violent content, they begin to do so at a very early age and their parents do not intervene.
- Many bullies have strong personalities, are reasonably popular, are confident and assertive, according to research from Scandinavia.
- Bullies have a need for attention, are dependent on the group for support and sometimes bully more extremely than intended to impress others.
- One study has suggested a relationship between being cruel to animals and bullying.
- While bullies may emerge from any class, family circumstance or level of advantage, studies have found that poverty, disadvantage and family instability create conditions that are conducive to aggressive, physical bullying.

Differences between girls and boys

Girls and boys begin life with similar life strategies which continue up to approximately two to three years of age. However, by three to four years of age more boys are bullies and are being bullied, partly because of the different manner in which we consciously or unconsciously treat boys and girls, accepting assertiveness and aggression in boys while actively discouraging them in girls.

The following differences have been found between bullying in boys and girls:

- Boys are three times more likely to bully than girls.

- Boys bully both girls and boys.
- Girls only tend to bully other girls.
- Physical bullying is popular amongst boys.
- Emotional bullying is practised by girls.
- Girls engage in manipulative schemes, such as spreading rumours, taking away a victim's 'best friend' or systematically turning everyone against her.
- Girls more often join in bullying others, particularly if they do not like them.
- Unlike boys, girls receive little support for bullying behaviour. This may be why they are more reluctant to admit to bullying and why it goes underground.

THE EFFECTS ON THE BULLY

While it may seem that being a bully guarantees status, prestige and power and may provide protection from being bullied by others, the truth is that being a bully is a problematic condition which is more likely to lead to unhappiness in life.

Bullies may end up being unable to sustain good relationships with their partners and children, especially if their only strategy to achieve what they want is the use of violence or the abuse of power. Research also shows that bullies may go on to become involved in crime.

Bullies also find that they become isolated and unpopular and that their bullying strategies are not appreciated in the workplace. Bullies who become employers may find themselves on the receiving end of suits for sexual harassment, unfair dismissal or for physical assault.

The bully is, therefore, someone who may be as much in need of psychological intervention as the victims of bullying. Other problems which they may experience include the following:

- Incurring the active dislike of other children. One study shows that most children dislike bullying and are uncomfortable about it occurring in their school.
- Wondering if they are really liked or whether other children pretend to like them out of fear.
- Envying those who are intellectually competent, favoured by teachers or who acquire good examination results.
- Having to protect their position as class bully from other challengers who might try to overthrow them.
- Worrying about the future. Bullies will often admit that while they know they currently have the upper hand, by the time the Leaving Certificate is over victims will be out of their grasp with, perhaps, more promising futures ahead.
- Getting into trouble at school. Some bullies challenge the authority of teachers and the school. In this way, they may incur the wrath of school personnel who become increasingly angry with their disruptive behaviour.
- Getting into conflict with parents, as bullying behaviours spread into relationships with other family members.

THE ROLE OF GANGS

Many bullies operate successfully because of the psychological support or the protection from retaliation afforded by gangs. They look to gangs for applause, muscle power and for support for their fragile egos.

Bullies in gangs can operate more thoroughly, more dangerously and more effectively than the bully who operates alone. Being attacked by an individual may be upsetting, but being confronted by the bully and accompanying gang is an overwhelmingly distressing experience.

The potential of gangs to cause serious physical injury should not be overlooked. Regardless of an individual's intelligence, self-esteem or even physical prowess, they are not sufficient to withstand the attack of a gang. As a result, it may well be dangerous to advise children to stick up for themselves.

Group behaviour also lends a semblance of accept-ability to even the most outrageous of abuses. Most of all, groups allow for the progressive desensitisation to the ef-fects of bullying on the victim by reassuring oneself that 'everyone else is involved'.

Furthermore, the gang can decide on the pop groups to be followed, the clothes to be worn or the records to be bought. Victims are isolated from these decisions.

Gangs can be used to spread rumours, to steal a vic-tim's friends or to organise activities to which the victim is not invited.

Gangs may also become cohesive and impenetrable. Stories are agreed on and members are protected. Conse-quently, a teacher trying to establish what has happened to a victim may be led to believe that nothing occurred or that the victim was the cause of the problem.

Likewise, parents enquiring about bullying are unlike-ly to dismiss the accounts of several children if there is con-sistency and plausibility between their accounts.

Therefore, gangs further isolate victims, ensuring that they cannot retaliate, that they cannot disclose what is hap-pening to them and that even if they do seek adult help their story will be outweighed by the majority account.

SPOTTING THE BULLY

Parents are frequently unaware that their child is a bully

and many are surprised, shocked, upset and distressed to discover that their child is responsible for bullying behaviour. This is partly because of the secretive, devious and covert nature of the problem. It is also because bullies have a vested interest in keeping their behaviour out of sight of authority.

Identifying the school bully, therefore, is a difficult task for parents. The following questions ought to be asked:

- Have remarks been made implying that your child has behaved badly or in a bullying manner?
- Have any formal complaints been received?
- Are other parents more wary of your child or have they ceased to issue invitations?
- Do friends phone, call to the door or avoid your child's company?
- Have you observed your child in any aggressive bullying behaviour?
- Have you overheard descriptions of school friends that were harsh, derogatory or cruel?
- Have you noticed possessions that you did not provide, money in excess of allowances or more sweets than would be expected?
- Were there incidents at home where the response of the child was particularly hurtful, vindictive, nasty or threatening?
- Does your child respond unsympathetically when other family members are hurt, upset or in trouble?
- Do brothers and sisters complain about bullying behaviour?
- Has your child ever been bullied either at home by a brother or sister or in school?
- Does the child respond to discipline with anger or with

normal compliance?

- How well does your child tolerate frustration, control temper or wait for something?
- Does your child choose excessively violent television programmes and videos, or laugh with enjoyment during scenes of violence?
- Does your child have academic or learning difficulties that might reduce self-confidence?
- Are there problems with homework? Are there complaints about school 'swots' or about other family members who work hard?
- Is there any physical deformity, disability or disfigurement that might cause defensiveness or anger?
- Has there been exposure to prejudice through extended family members who hold strong views about colour, class or creed?
- How does your child talk about the aged, the poor, the disabled?
- Is there any apparent cruelty to animals?
- Has overly-harsh or overly-permissive discipline been a feature of family life?
- Has there been inconsistency in discipline or more attention given to brothers and sisters?
- Have there been family difficulties, such as illness, death, financial problems, problems of marital discord, separation or violence that were upsetting or during which the child received little attention?

STEPS TO TAKE

As much as we need to help the victims of bullying, so too do children who are bullies need intervention and psychological support. The following is some advice for parents:

- Establish without doubt that the child has been bullying.
- Do not rush in with harsh words, physical punishments or threats. This would be a demonstration of bullying, which is the behaviour you wish to challenge.
- Visit the school and seek their knowledge and understanding of the problem. Find out if other children are involved. Establish if any sanctions from the school are forthcoming.
- Establish if your child is a bully or both a bully and victim. However, try to get independent evidence as well as the child's own account.
- Speak to your partner and decide on a united, consistent and reasonable approach to the problem.
- Express your concern to the child that they would behave in a bullying manner.
- Try to find out if anxiety, school problems or other worries caused the bullying.
- Try to establish whether any family problems might have contributed to the bullying.
- Insist that the child takes responsibility for bullying behaviour and, if appropriate, apologises.
- Find out if rewards were obtained by bullying.
- Ensure that money, goods and belongings taken from other children are returned.
- Ensure that any malicious damage is repaired and that the child pays for repairs.
- Establish what is necessary for the school to accept that the bullying is over. Decide how you will work with the school on this matter.
- Consider a change of school for the child, either to remove them from a bullying gang or to allow them to 'turn over a new leaf' in a new environment.

- Ascertain if the child has any unidentified intellectual, academic or learning problems or if too much pressure for achievement may have affected their behaviour.
- Reassure the child of your love and support in overcoming the problem.
- If the bullying is of a sustained, intense and serious nature and the child appears unable or unwilling to address the problem, seek professional help.

ADVICE FOR TEACHERS

Teachers are often rendered powerless to intervene on behalf of children who are being bullied. They themselves may also be the target of bullying.

Teachers are expected to monitor, address and arrest the problem of students bullying each other in school. Furthermore, teachers are called upon to deal with the bullies and victims, including irate parents. They may also be subjected to the following:

- They may be blamed if they accuse a child of bullying.
- They may be threatened with violence or litigation if they suspend or expel a pupil.
- They may be blamed if they do not intervene to stop the bullying.
- They may be legally threatened if they fail to protect a child from physical or emotional assault.
- They may become targets for violent assault.

It is no wonder, therefore, that many teachers become overwhelmed by the stress of school life and by the trauma of coping with bullying behaviour.

SPOTTING THE VICTIMS

The skills which a teacher requires in dealing with bullying are many and varied. They need skills to communicate with parents, other teachers, the school principal, legal advisors and outside agencies such as the school's psychological service, the health services, community welfare officers and the police.

More importantly, they need skills to communicate with pupils and to identify those who are bullied and the bullies themselves.

A survey of Irish children victimised in primary school showed that 65% had not informed their teachers. It is not clear if this reluctance is because children do not want to 'rat' on the bullies, because they see no benefit to informing their teachers or because teachers are not creating the climate in which a child can tell in safety.

Furthermore, when children have told their teachers, they have not always been helped. One Irish study showed that almost two-thirds of teachers at second level are perceived by their students as being non-interventionist when it comes to bullying.

However, Irish studies have also shown that 84% of second level students do not tell their teachers that they are being bullied. Teachers, therefore, may be left unaware of the extent of bullying in their class or school and may also be unaware of the need to intervene more often or more vigorously.

The fact that so few pupils disclose being bullied leaves the teacher with the task of identifying victims. The following may be helpful in identifying those who need teacher support:

- Note any dramatic change in the student's behaviour. A victim who is bullied because of being good may decide to behave badly instead.
- Look out for a pattern of being late for school or class. Victims often intentionally arrive late to avoid being bullied en route.
- Be alert to a deterioration in school performance. Victims who are bullied because of being intellectually or

academically advanced often feign ignorance.

- Note if a student has an excess of lost or forgotten homework. It could be that the homework has been stolen, hidden or thrashed beyond repair. This is a common bullying strategy.
- Be vigilant for comments, sniggering, ridicule or remarks which are directed towards a student during class.
- Check if there is anyone with whom others will not talk, sit beside or share a book during class.
- Read class essays to identify possible messages about being bullied. In one instance, a child who attempted suicide had written about his despair in an essay the previous week.
- Examine drawings done by younger children for signs of being bullied. A tiny figure representing the child surrounded by large figures representing classmates may be significant. Similarly, a figure alone and away from others would be a cause for concern.
- Occasionally arrive early to the classroom and observe the students who are being picked on.
- Watch out for groups of children that exclude a particular student.
- Observe if a student lingers after class and is fearful of being far from adult company.
- Notice if a child lingers around you in the playground.
- Observe if a student has an excess of minor cuts, abrasions, bruises or bandages. One child reported having a hand dragged the length of a wall until it was bleeding.
- Observe the playground from an overlooking window, if possible. Bullying that is hidden or absorbed in the noise and chaos of the playground is easier to spot

from a height.

- Watch out for students who are exceptionally shy, retiring, anxious or sensitive.
- Be sensitive to a student who appears to be unhappy, sighing, frozen, wary, nervous or close to tears.
- Remember that all students who have a physical or an academic disability may be more at risk of being bullied.
- Remember that children who are developmentally different or who look and sound different are often bullied.
- Be alert to the different physiques of children. Studies show that many victims of bullying are of physically weaker stature.
- Be aware of the clumsy student who performs poorly at sports.
- Note other attributes that might make a student more vulnerable, such as poor personal hygiene and personal habits.
- In a non-uniform school, observe the student who has notably less clothes or clothes that are particularly unfashionable. Girls, particularly, can bully others because of a difference in dress.
- Express clear disdain for bullying behaviour and your unconditional support for bullying victims. In this way, you may not need to identify victims; they may identify themselves to you.

SPOTTING THE BULLIES

Few bullies come to a teacher's immediate attention. Many have Jekyll and Hyde personalities, transforming themselves into bullies in the playground or out of the view of adults.

Bullying, by its nature, is a secretive, covert activity which is often ingeniously hidden from adult eyes. Additionally, a bully does not belong to a single 'category' or 'type' that allows for easy identification, nor is bullying behaviour consistent in amount, intensity or duration.

The following are some tips on how to identify bullies at school:

- Be aware of any family circumstances, such as a bereavement or parental separation, that may have occurred. Some children bully as a response to traumatic events that they cannot handle.
- Assess what you know about a student's background. For example, consider any punitive or harsh discipline at home. This style of parenting is often displaced by the bully on to others.
- Note that a student who reacts to correction with frustration or aggression may also react aggressively to others.
- Look out for group leaders who are aggressive, who swagger and who are show-offs. Their status may have been achieved by intimidation rather than by admiration.
- Be alert to pupils who express snide or negative remarks about others. They may also manifest bullying behaviour.
- Be alert to the attitudes expressed by students. For example, listen for remarks that are cruel or that are dismissive of other people's feelings.
- Be aware of students with poor academic skill, who may try to recoup self-esteem through bullying.
- Remember that one of the warning signs of bullying is cruelty to animals.

- Be alert to remarks that are sexist, discriminatory or harassing. These are bullying remarks and the perpetrators are bullies.
- Patrol areas where bullying is likely to occur. You may catch the bully in the act.

DEALING WITH BULLIES

Teachers cannot be expected to deal effectively with bullies unless there is a clear, written and unambiguous bullying policy in the school which is agreed between parents, teachers and the children themselves.

Even when a bullying code exists, it can still be difficult to determine if an incident is a true case of bullying. For example, a teacher may be uncertain whether a physical row is a squabble amongst equals or a case of bullying. Additionally, a teacher may mistake the retaliation of a victim for the attack of a bully.

Furthermore, it can be difficult to evaluate bullying incidents. Is this the first time that the child has bullied or the first time the child was caught? Is the bullying mild or severe, careless or cruel, retaliatory or aggressive? Was there destruction of property, extortion, blackmail, emotional or physical assault? Is the child a good pupil, a disruptive pupil, a person who behaves aggressively, a person who is usually kind, a person going through a crisis at home or a child who has a long history of behavioural problems?

Teachers are also concerned by ethical considerations, including how to be just, fair and objective in assessing incidents of bullying.

Given the complexity of the problem, the following may help teachers who need to confront a bully:

- Make it clear to the bully that either you or others have

observed their bullying behaviour.

- Do not tell a bully that the victim has complained.
- Ask the bully to give an account of what happened.
- Let the bully know that you are writing down their account. Read it back and ask that it be confirmed as the account you were given. Provide an opportunity for the account to be reconsidered or revised.
- Ask the bully for the names of any witnesses to the incident. Note their names and inform the bully that they will be interviewed separately.
- Make sure that the bully has no opportunity to meet witnesses, particularly if they are either part of a bullying gang or victims who could be intimidated.
- Ask the bully for a definition of bullying behaviour and ask if the incident meets that definition.
- Enquire how the bully's parents are likely to respond to the incident.

Questions, such as the following, may also be useful:

1. *How do you feel now: sad, angry, happy, guilty, annoyed?*
2. *Who do you think was most upset by the fight?*
3. *Who do you think was most physically hurt?*
4. *Do you think it was an equal fight?*
5. *Would your friends say it was an equal fight?*
6. *Who do you blame for what happened?*
7. *Who do you think other people will blame?*

Finally, if the school has a bullying code, inform the bully in age-appropriate terms how the code may have been breached. Tell the bully that investigations will continue, that parents will be notified and that agreed sanctions may be imposed. Reassure the bully of your help to overcome the bullying behaviour.

DEALING WITH THE BULLY'S PARENTS

Bullying often causes parents and teachers to blame each other. Teachers may believe that bullying is learned behaviour, acquired by observing or experiencing domineering, abusive or violent interactions in the home. Parents, in turn, may accuse teachers of favouritism, discrimination or picking on certain children.

Parents may also blame teachers for not being vigilant about bullying. Teachers, in turn, complain that parents often act in an aggressive, denying and threatening manner when their child is identified as a bully.

Either way, teachers and the parents of bullies will need to meet and discuss the allegations being made and establish how the problem can be resolved.

The following are some guidelines for teachers:

- Invite the parents to the school to discuss a breach of school bullying policy.
- Do not discuss the incident on the phone. Reassure the parents that there will be an opportunity for full discussion once the meeting takes place.
- Interview the parents, if possible, in the presence of the school principal or a colleague who is aware of the problem.
- Begin with a summary of the school's bullying code and emphasis the parents' agreement to it.
- If the school does not have a bullying code, try to establish the parents' views and awareness of school bullying.
- Inform the parents in a clear, unemotional, unambiguous and non-judgmental manner of the evidence you have that their child has bullied. List times, dates, number of witnesses and how conclusions were reached.

- Sympathise with the parents about how upsetting and worrying it can be if a child is caught bullying and ask for their reaction.
- Ask the parents for their views on what caused their child to behave in this way. For example, could a recent illness, family bereavement, new arrival or other circumstance have upset their child?
- Inform the parents of the sanctions that the school considers appropriate and enlist their cooperation.
- Be sympathetic towards parents who deny that their child could have bullied, but remind them of the long-term dangers to their child if the behaviour goes unchecked.
- Seek the parents' help in communicating the seriousness of the incident to the bully. Draw up a contract between parents, school and bully about future behavioural requirements, how they will be monitored and how the bully will be punished if the agreement is not adhered to.
- Establish with the parents if professional help is required by their child. Find out if the problem arose because of a learning difficulty, pressure for achievement, a family crisis or any other emotional disturbance. Assist the parents in securing a referral to the appropriate agency.
- Be aware of family situations where excessive discipline could result from notifying parents of their child's behaviour. In these instances, consultation with professionals on how to approach the problem may be necessary.

DEALING WITH VICTIMS

Those who have been bullied have often lost their confidence. Older children, particularly, will be vulnerable and sensitive about their status as a victim. Therefore, while many will be happy to know that they will be protected from being bullied, they may resist attempts to elicit their emotional reactions to the experience.

The school is a far from ideal location for therapy and teachers should not be expected to undertake that task. If therapy is required, a referral to a psychologist or psychiatrist, which is made with the consent of parents, is recommended.

Therefore, the teacher's role in helping victims is primarily one of reassurance while enabling the student to progress at school, safe and secure from bullying. The following advice may be helpful:

- If the victim has disclosed the problem to you, praise their courage in doing so.
- Reassure the victim that being bullied is the responsibility of bullies and that victims are not to blame.
- Reassure the victim of your continuing support and help in ensuring that it does not happen again.
- Make arrangements to meet at regular intervals to discuss how the problem is going.
- Ascertain who in the victim's class is likely to be antagonistic and establish the safeguards required by the victim to feel secure in the future.

The following questions may also be helpful in interviews with a victim of bullying:

1. *Who is the most friendly to you in your class?*
2. *Who likes the bullies? Who dislikes bullying?*
3. *Who stood up for you or who would like to have helped you*

when you were being bullied?

4. *Would you like an opportunity to let the bully know what it felt like to be bullied?*
5. *How much has your school-work suffered because you were bullied?*
6. *How do you think that the bully will behave now towards you?*
7. *What would help to make things easier?*
8. *Does anything else need to happen for you to know that school is safe again?*
9. *If anyone tried to bully you in the future, who would you talk to about it?*

The answers to the above questions will help the teacher to select supportive children from the class who might assist the victim. They will also identify class members who are either tolerant of bullying or whose behaviour towards the victim may require monitoring.

DEALING WITH THE VICTIM'S PARENTS
The response of the victim's parents may be one of shock, guilt, anger, relief or distress depending on whether they had any previous suspicions or knowledge that their child was being bullied. The following may be helpful when dealing with parents:

- Invite the parents to discuss bullying in the school.
- Do not enter into discussion on the phone.
- At the meeting, inform the parents of their child's disclosure or of your discovery of bullying.
- Inform them of all the steps that have been taken so far.
- Make the parents aware of the conversations you have had with their child about what has happened and

about future strategies to ensure that no repetition occurs.

- If any feature in the child, such as poor personal habits, annoying behaviour or lack of social skills contributed to being bullied, discuss them sensitively with the parents.
- Discuss the benefits of referral for professional help.
- Reassure the parents of your continued support and vigilance and suggest follow-up meetings with the parents to review the situation.
- In cases where parents are angry or blaming the school, acknowledge their upset, repeat the school policy on bullying and outline the steps taken to assist their child.
- Do not take it personally if the parents decide to remove the child from the school. They may wish to provide the child with a fresh start.

IMPLEMENTING ANTI-BULLYING POLICIES

It is difficult for schools to operate without a clearly defined, visible and agreed code of behaviour with regard to bullying. Such a code would usually include the following:

- Agreed definitions of bullying, in addition to clear boundaries and rules for behaviour.
- Methods for investigating any report of bullying.
- Agreed strategies for responding to each bullying event.
- Monitoring of high-risk times for bullying and also of physical locations in which bullying is likely to occur.
- Assigning teachers and prefects to detect bullying.
- Setting up systems to reward non-bullying behaviour in the school.
- Providing information on bullying through class discussion, seminars and video presentations.

- Providing a support system for victims and a non-aggressive approach to bullies.
- Providing a support system for school staff.

Some countries, such as Norway, have had national anti-bullying campaigns for many years. Others, such as Sweden, have anti-bullying programmes which place responsibility for tackling the problem on school principals.

In Ireland, in 1993, The Department of Education issued *Guidelines for Countering Bullying Behaviour in Primary and Post-Primary Schools.* These guidelines recommend that schools address the problem of bullying as part of their code of discipline and they outline the consultation process to be used in formulating anti-bullying codes.

The following is a summary of the many national anti-bullying policies and the strategies they employ:

- Administering annual questionnaires to monitor bullying levels in schools.
- Establishing student councils, which are elected by pupils to safeguard their interests.
- Introducing a 'buddy' system, which involves assigning carefully selected pupils as protectors of younger or more vulnerable students.
- Establishing 'bully courts'. These courts, which include pupils, judge behaviour and prescribe sanctions for bullying.
- Assigning a network of professionals to assist schools and to provide information packs on bullying for teachers, parents and students. This was the basis of the Norwegian campaign.
- Using dramatic illustrations. The Sticks and Stones Theatre Company is an Irish theatre company which

presents the horrors of bullying in dramatic form, tailoring their demonstrations to the needs of individual schools.

- Providing specialist research facilities. The Anti-Bullying Research and Resource Centre, Trinity College, Dublin, is an information, research, consultation and counselling resource available to schools in Ireland.
- Developing specific policies, such as the 'whole school', anti-bullying programme devised in the UK. This programme includes a written document outlining the steps and procedures to be followed in the event of bullying. It also includes classroom activities to raise awareness of bullying, assertiveness courses for victims, as well as peer counselling and training for staff on how to monitor the school playground.
- Adopting a 'community approach'. This takes account of the wider community and the role played by people like parents, non-teaching staff, bus drivers and police in monitoring and countering bullying behaviour.

Research suggests that vigorous, concerted, sustained and cooperative implementation of policies to combat bullying in schools is effective in significantly reducing school bullying. Unfortunately, research also concludes that without concerted intervention, children will continue to conceal their experiences of being bullied at school and bullies will continue their reign of terror against them.

BULLYING AT WORK

Just as the child must go to school, so also has the adult a need to go to work. Just like school, the adult enters an enclosed, hierarchical environment where the bullied may believe that they are obliged to take what is handed out by others and feel that there is no escape.

So great is the problem of bullying in the workplace that an estimated 30%–50% of stress-related illness may be caused by people being bullied at work. European estimates of bullying indicate that as many as 12 million workers suffer psychological violence in the workplace.

The impact of bullying is so serious that 20% of male suicides have been attributed to bullying, according to one Swedish study. A Norwegian study found that 40% of those who were bullied had considered suicide. Therefore, it would seem that for a substantial number of victims, being bullied makes their lives so miserable that killing themselves becomes the only means of escape.

Of course, survey results vary widely and depend on how bullying is defined and the extent to which a particular country or culture tackles the problem. As a result, estimates of the extent of workplace bullying range from 25%–50% of employees. However, Sweden, where the pioneering work on bullying has been carried out and which now has anti-bullying legislation in place, has the lowest reported incidence of workplace bullying at 3.5%.

A 1994 British survey found that more than 50% of respondents expressed that they had been bullied at work at one time, with the younger (under 25 years) and more vulnerable workers accounting for close to 70% of those bullied. Another British study, in 1996, found that one in every eight was a victim of bullying and the majority of perpetrators in that study were department heads and senior executives.

Like all abuses of power, bullying thrives on secrecy, shame, intimidation and fear and most studies indicate substantial under-reporting. As a consequence, precise figures for workplace bullying in this country are not available. However, current research and extrapolations from international statistics indicate that it is a problem of significant dimensions. For example, Irish interviews with victims of workplace bullying, which were conducted by The Anti-Bullying Research and Resource Centre at Trinity College, Dublin, indicated that 64% had contemplated suicide 'as a means to end their suffering'. Furthermore, a survey by the Irish Nurses' Organisation found that 95% of nurses had been bullied at some stage in their careers.

THE OPPORTUNITIES FOR WORKPLACE BULLYING

The workplace provides one of the ideal breeding-grounds for bullying behaviour because of the formalised power relationships and hierarchies that are established there and the power structures that exist within work organisations. Supervision, managerial control and the differentiation between different ranks within a company, create an environment in which people exercise the trappings of power over others. Bullying problems arise when individuals abuse that power by bringing to bear on the workplace their value judgements, personal prejudices, experiences, inadequacies or psychological stresses.

The very nature of the language that surrounds work also invites bullying behaviour. Consider the casual use of common workplace words such as *superiors, subordinates, higher ranks, rank and file, managers, seniors, juniors,* all of which imply that some people are exalted while others are of lesser value. It is not difficult to identify which of the above would be more likely to be bullied. Allied to this vocabulary is the practice whereby people are often graded on numerical scales of worth. In this milieu, the workplace holds the potential for bullying to arise in the following ways:

- Males in dominant positions may abuse females, a greater proportion of whom hold lower-grade, part-time positions.
- Workers of strong character may abuse those who are weaker in the day-to-day allocation of work or privileges.
- Instructions may be issued to employees in a disrespectful or demeaning manner.
- Work may be evaluated, performance assessed or skills vetted in a way that constitutes bullying.
- Meetings may be called, policies decided on and decisions taken in a manner which excludes certain individuals.
- Favours may be dispensed, opportunities for overtime scheduled and promotions allocated based on discriminatory bullying treatment.
- Holiday times may be allocated, pay and conditions decided, lunch hours assigned in a manner where fairness is disregarded.
- Unattainable productivity or sales targets may be set for selected employees.
- Role specification may be poorly defined, ever-changing and unattainable, so that one is never sure if they are doing what is required because what is required is unclear.

- Work allocation may be unfairly distributed. For example, a person may be given excessive work or excessive responsibility or, alternatively, the workload may be reduced to a point where the employee feels redundant.
- Unfair criteria may be used in the way that physical space in an office building is allocated, offices are distributed or withheld, partitions between work stations are erected or the manner in which desks are assigned in sunlight or draughts.
- People may be situated far away from facilities, coffee machines, canteens, toilets or at the top of the building, under the eye of a supervisor or with little dignity or privacy.
- Unjust or unfair rules may be used in the way that rewards are granted, prizes for achieving sales quotas are awarded, trips abroad are allocated, Christmas bonuses are dispensed, seminar attendees are selected or staff representatives are chosen.

Regardless of whether one is the victim of discriminatory behaviour or the casualty of bullying, most work situations share the condition that *you can't walk out*. It is this condition of being trapped, regardless of what is being perpetrated, that causes the experience of being bullied to be so emotionally and physically damaging to the health, safety, sanity and self-esteem of employees.

WHY PEOPLE FEEL TRAPPED

Perhaps the most crucial factor explaining the intense depression and misery caused by workplace bullying is that most people feel trapped in their place of work. As a result, work may be experienced as a life sentence, where one is condemned, on a daily basis, to stress, harassment, embarrassment, insult, injustice, overwork, belittlement, discrimination or gross subjugation to the prejudices, manipulations or inadequacies of others. Whether a person has the ability to leave or remain in their job depends on many factors. The following is a list of the factors involved:

- Lack of financial independence. Men, in particular, are often trapped by being the primary or sole financial support for their family.
- Difficulty finding alternative employment because of age, or finding oneself without sufficient qualifications to be hired elsewhere.
- Fearing change and the fear of having to start all over again.
- Fearing that a position of similar status might not be attained elsewhere.
- Hoping that the problem might disappear, or that the bully might be transferred or might move on.
- Worries about the inconvenience of travelling to a new location or about the extra expense incurred by shifting from a local to a more distant job.
- Fears that domestic arrangements would be disrupted. In particular, women working part-time may put up with workplace bullying because a change in employment might not accord with crèche hours, nursery school hours or child-minding arrangements.
- Deep-seated fear that one is responsible for being bullied.
- Fear of recurrence of the problem in the next work situation.
- Concern about getting a reference.
- Belief that one has no other talents.

- Feelings of weakness, shame and inadequacy.
- Worry about loss of pension or other rights.
- Inability to discuss the problem with others or to seek guidance about one's options.

SYMPTOMS OF BEING BULLIED AT WORK

The experience of being bullied at work evokes a range of emotions, behaviours and social changes in the person who is bullied. The following are some examples:

- Fear of going to work.
- Monday morning depression and Friday evening elation.
- Feeling unhappy, depressed, helpless and hopeless, entertaining thoughts of suicide.
- Experiencing anxiety and feelings of panic in anticipation of the day's work ahead.
- Feeling ill, fatigued, unable to cope, finding that one's immunity to illness has decreased, being absent from work more often due to minor and irritating complaints.
- Experiencing both anger and helplessness simultaneously.
- Making errors due to loss of confidence or due to fear of being observed or reprimanded.
- Rushing work so as not to incur the wrath of the bully.
- Watching the clock and praying for the day to end.
- Trying to be inconspicuous in executing daily tasks.
- Avoiding situations that might draw the attention of the bully or that require consulting or being in the presence of the bully.
- Being unwilling to participate in work activities.
- Avoiding work-related social activities.

- Going out for lunch rather than using the canteen.
- Not joining colleagues for a drink after work.
- Suffering from burnout, which is defined as 'a progressive loss of idealism, energy, purpose and concern as a result of conditions of work'.

THE PERPETRATORS OF WORKPLACE BULLYING

The perpetrators of bullying at work tend to share common psychological features. These include an inability to respect the rights and dignity of others, deep-seated insecurity which finds expression in the wielding of power over others and anxiety which is often revealed in ingratiating behaviour towards their own managers.

Emotional immaturity, which reveals itself in outbursts of temper, is a common feature in bullies. Bullies also often have an intense fear of criticism, constantly shifting blame on to their subordinates and showing an inability to accept or admit to their own limitations.

The psychological profile of the bully often reveals early life experiences that involved harsh punishment and feelings of helplessness and rage. They have been brought up to believe that 'might is right', are often fiercely competitive or devious in their early and adolescent years, and frequently inherit the racist, sexist or ageist prejudices of their parents.

The workplace bully may have a long history of bullying others in school, a history of cowardice, an enjoyment of hurting others and they may experience amusement and power through the humiliation of other people.

One category of bully is found amongst the Type A personality, although not all Type A personalities are bullies. The characteristics of the Type A personality include being highly competitive, driven, hostile, work-obsessed, thriving on pressure and deadlines, unable to delegate, achievement-oriented, urgent, needing to be in control, anxious for approval of superiors, inflexible, rigid, impatient, unable to relax, having poor ability to laugh at oneself and easily provoked when challenged.

Clinical work with bullies shows that they often employ the psychological processes known as 'defence mechanisms'. These are unconscious processes that reduce anxiety in the following manner:

Rationalisation – justifying bullying on the grounds that employees would otherwise abuse the system.

Denial – involves the blocking or denial of the act of bullying.

Repression – convenient forgetting of bullying outbursts or of irrational behaviour.

Sublimation – diverting anxiety, anger, disappointment into work achievement.

Projection – attributing personal prejudices, envy, jealousies, faults and problems to other people. For example, the boss who is threatened by the creativity, innovative ability or skill of an employee may insist that the reality is the reverse. Sometimes, a bully may even accuse victims of anger or paranoia and project their feelings on to them.

Just as there are common features in the background and psychological profiles of bullies, so too are there differences in what causes one person to bully another. Types of bullies may include the following:

The ideological bullies, who work from the belief that staff will take unfair advantage if not coerced into working hard.

The reactive bullies, who have had their kindness taken advantage of in the past and who are determined to provide no latitude to staff.

The inadequate bullies, who require the subjugation of others to enhance their feeling of importance.

The perverted bullies, who enjoy inflicting pain and suffering on others.

The cowardly bullies, who target the weak, vulnerable and insecure, while proffering charm to peers and superiors.

The defensive bullies, who fear their own lack of competence, creativity, ability, sociability, and are envious and threatened by anyone who is talented. These bullies constitute a substantial portion of the bullying population.

The hierarchical bullies, who find themselves being bullied from above and who displace their anger and frustration on to the next in line.

The immature bullies, who have temper tantrums when things do not go their way.

The insidious bullies, who quietly torment their victims through intangible gibes, irritations, changing demands, subtle changes in work allocation, providing misinformation, setting impossible deadlines, generating work overload or removing responsibility.

The isolating bullies, whose victims are cut off from clients or colleagues and who ensure that invitations to business meetings, social events, courses and seminars are no longer issued.

The defamatory bullies, who systematically erode a person's good name through innuendo, body-language, slips of the tongue and subterfuge.

The paranoid bullies, who search desks or personal belongings, eavesdrop on telephone conversations, maintain close physical proximity and control all material such as stamps, pens and paper.

A substantial number of people who seek therapy because they are being bullied at work will describe the perpetrator as someone who fits into one of the above categories.

THE CASUALTIES OF WORKPLACE BULLYING

Just as workplace bullies may share some common early histories, personal traits and life experiences, so too may the casualties of bullying reveal common characteristics. Research on the casualties of workplace bullying has identified certain individuals as being more likely to be bullied. These include the following:

- Intellectually superior employees who have not achieved positions commensurate with their ability. They may serve as a threat to less intellectually able managers.
- Creative and innovative employees with a wealth of new ideas and projects.
- Workers who achieve high productivity, thereby threatening their inadequate superiors.
- Employees who are young, attractive, stylish and enthusiastic.
- Workaholics who irritate, frustrate or threaten others by their extreme meticulousness and conscientiousness.
- Employees who have social, class or financial advantages not shared by other members of the workforce. Women whose partners or husbands have high social status or wealth are a good example.
- Workers who seem to achieve with ease, to be lucky or to be 'blessed with success'.

- Socially skilled, popular and admired workers who attract the attention of others.
- Socially unskilled workers, who are poor communicators, who invade personal space and who do not read body-language well.
- Employees whose shyness makes others uncomfortable or tense.
- The very young or the elderly.
- Those with a different sexual orientation.
- Employees who are suffering from life crises such as marital separation, divorce or family problems.
- Those who are suffering from bereavement or who are grieving the end of relationships.
- Those who are pregnant, going on maternity leave or returning from work leave.

The casualties of bullying thus tend to be divided into the very able, intelligent and advantaged and the less able, poorly socially skilled and vulnerable.

WORK WHICH FACILITATES BULLYING

Certain types of work lend themselves to bullying behaviour, either because the work is innately stressful, the clientele threatening or assaultive (such as in police, prison or security work), the structures rigid (such as in the defence forces), or the work and goals limited and circumscribed.

The following are some examples of work where stress and bullying may be facilitated:

- Where supervision is required.
- Where there is very little independence, where team work is essential and where there is considerable scrutiny, such as in an operating theatre.

- Where meticulous attention to detail is required, such as in the law or accountancy.
- Where the work is highly stressful, such as in bomb disposal, crowd control or flying planes.
- Where conditions are crowded and where people are physically cramped.
- Where critical decisions have to be made quickly, such as in the fire brigade, ambulance service, hospital casualty or in a stock exchange.
- Where deadlines operate, such as in the media.
- Where customers are likely to be angry or aggrieved, such as in hospital waiting-rooms where people are anxious, frightened or in pain.
- Where there may be disappointment for customers, such as in a housing department or in a labour exchange.
- Where sales targets have to be met and onerous targets are set.
- Where staff are exposed to human suffering, such as in health care where they may experience feelings of helplessness about their ability to alleviate the problems of patients.
- Where the work is potentially dangerous, such as transporting cash, driving buses or working in the rescue services.

PERSONAL CONSEQUENCES OF WORKPLACE BULLYING

There are many consequences that may result from bullying at work. It is not anticipated that any one individual would experience all of the following, but at least some are likely to be encountered:

- Problems in concentration.
- Reduced powers of observation.

- Increase in distractibility.
- Increase in errors or in judgement.
- Loss of confidence in making decisions.
- Loss of memory.
- Reduced intellectual reasoning.
- Impaired ability to absorb, retain or retrieve information.
- Behaving distractedly, carelessly or dangerously.
- General clumsiness, breaking objects, falling and tripping more.
- Problems in handling equipment.
- Eating hurriedly.
- Problems of time management, general disorganisation and problems carrying out tasks.
- Absence from work or facing constructive dismissal.
- Touchiness, irritability, hostility, defensiveness.
- Constant ruminations and obsessive thoughts about work.
- Impulsive or irrational behaviour.
- Feelings of anxiety and panic.
- Sensitivity, defensiveness.
- Emotional outbursts.
- Lowering of spirits, feelings of powerlessness, depression.
- Loss of self-esteem.
- Tearfulness, sadness, looking sad, feeling miserable.
- Becoming obsessed with fantasies of revenge.
- Increased tendency to criticise.
- Increased use of caffeine, alcohol, tobacco or other substances.
- Sleep patterns disrupted, with problems either in falling asleep, staying asleep or with waking exceptionally early in the morning.

- Fatigue or bouts of sudden and unusual tiredness.
- Vague and poorly-defined aches and pains and general malaise.
- Medical problems, such as hypertension, digestive problems, ulcers, coronary heart disease.
- Psychological ill-health or mental breakdown.
- Migraine, skin diseases, pre-menstrual tension, sexual impotence and sexual problems, back problems, and many other medical conditions.

RESOLVING THE PROBLEM

Tackling bullying at work necessitates building up one's own psychological resistance to being bullied, diluting the impact by ensuring that one has a full and fulfilling life outside work, learning stress management techniques to reduce the physiological and medical impact of being bullied, acquiring powers of assertiveness, becoming skilled in conflict management and acquainting oneself with relevant legislation and one's rights and duties at an organisational level.

The following suggestions may be helpful:

- Before making any complaint about bullying, ensure that you are genuinely being bullied and not overreacting, taking offence or challenging or resisting normal work requirements.
- Ensure that you are not displacing stress from outside of work on to your relationships at work.
- Ensure that you are not being over-sensitive, touchy or irritable and that the situation is one which witnesses would genuinely agree is a problem of bullying.
- Remember that an isolated incident of aggressive behaviour by a manager may not be grounds for a com-

plaint of bullying. By its very nature, bullying is usually repetitive, intentional, selective and progressive.

- Having established the above, do not be afraid to address any genuine experience of bullying and to respond vigorously until a successful conclusion is achieved.
- Keep a meticulous record of all the incidents in which you were bullied, the actual words used and the manner in which the encounter was concluded.
- Compose a list of the privileges to which you had previously been entitled, such as business lunches, social events, seminars and courses, and the invitations that have been withdrawn or the requests that have been denied since the bullying began.
- Take a note of your punctuality, your coffee breaks and lunch breaks and your daily work schedule so that you have a detailed account of your work commitment.
- Contact others in the organisation who might support you in your claim of unfair treatment.
- If the person who is bullying you previously worked in another department or another employment, try to establish if bullying had also occurred there.
- Retain all references and reviews from previous employers or reviews from your current work organisation, which pre-date the bullying. These will attest to your competence and ability and may challenge defamatory accounts.
- Anticipate the manner in which the bully finds fault and avoid it. For example, be more than punctual or find out about all meetings that you are expected to attend.
- If you have innovative ideas, send an official memo to the bully and copies to the bully's superiors. This will

ensure that the bully does not take the credit for your creativity. Taking credit for the intellect or creativity of victims is a very common practice of bullies and it is estimated that approximately two-thirds of bullying arises through envy.

- Seek official support. Consult your union and acquaint yourself with your rights and duties as an employee and the rights and duties of your employer.

- Inquire if your organisation has a policy on bullying and, if so, note the manner in which the bully has contravened that policy.

- Establish your company's complaints procedure and follow it to the letter.

- Make a formal request in writing for an appointment with the manager to whom you wish to present your problem. Make it known when requesting the appointment that the situation to be discussed is serious and be well-prepared for the meeting.

- Do not ask for immediate action or an immediate response. This may be threatening to the person to whom you make the complaint. Acquaint them fully with your case and let them know that you await their considered response within the following weeks.

THINGS TO AVOID

- Don't rush your complaint or make unsubstantiated claims. Gather evidence of incidents, times and dates, names of witnesses, names of other victims or any written material, memos or documents that may indicate the degree of bullying.

- Don't make broad, general complaints. For example, if you are being overworked or faced with unrealistic deadlines, detail the work, when it was given, what would be required to complete it and present this documentation. This is much more effective than complaining about being 'overworked', which provides the bully with the opportunity to accuse you of 'laziness'.

- Don't complain at a personal level or behave emotionally when making the complaint. In particular, don't focus complaints around your feelings, the personality of the bully or your personal reaction. Instead, detail your allegations in the context of the department, the company and your own productivity and work satisfaction.

- Do not attend any meetings without being properly prepared, and consider being represented at union or at legal level.

- Avoid ill-health and increased vulnerability. Make yourself as psychologically strong and resistant as possible by undertaking healthy activities, obtaining the support of your family and ensuring that you have sufficient relaxation time and techniques to carry you through.

- Do not expose yourself to the prospect of endangering your relationships or your sanity. If there is no redress, seek guidance about pursuing an alternative career.

SEXUAL BULLYING

Sexual bullying may arise where there is contact between males and females and where there is an abuse of power by one person over another. It is potent because of its potential to embarrass, demean, humiliate, undermine and cause distress, most often for the amusement, satisfaction or sense of control it provides offenders.

Power differentials between males and females and the traditional stereotype of dominant male and subordinate female often provide the necessary forum for the exercise of sexual bullying. The bullying behaviour arises because of the ignorance, inadequacies, cowardice, envy, resentment, the need for dominance or the vindictiveness of the perpetrator. While sexual bullying may occur in many contexts, the most frequent site is the workplace because it provides all the necessary conditions for abuses of power.

In recent decades, the rights and protection of men and women at work regarding sexual harassment, discrimination and bullying have received much attention. In 1977, the rights of the individual to protection from discrimination on grounds of their sex was affirmed through the Employment Equality Act of that year. In 1985, the right of an employee to freedom from sexual harassment was established as a condition of employment. Furthermore, both sexual harassment and bullying have not only been recognised as a problem but are now also being clearly defined and delineated in all their multiple manifestations.

WHAT IS SEXUAL BULLYING?

There are many definitions of sexual bullying, all of which

include an emphasis on the *repeated, persistent, unwelcomed and unwanted* nature of the sexual advances. All definitions recognise the range of verbal innuendo, offensive visual displays and actual physical contact that may constitute sexual harassment. All definitions recognise the degrading and offensive nature of the problem.

Sexual bullying may be subtle and insidious, such as a glance, an 'accidental' brushing past or too close a stance. Alternatively, it may be blatant and challenging, such as requesting sexual favours in return for keeping one's job or obtaining promotion. It may be annoying or traumatic. It may range from unwanted glances or advances to serious sexual assaults, such as rape.

What distinguishes an isolated, ill-considered, unintentional remark or touch from real harassment is the deliberate and repeated nature of the offence committed and the fact that it is committed in the full knowledge that it is embarrassing, insulting, intimidating or threatening to another individual.

Sexual bullying may take many forms, including the following:

- Sexual jokes and salacious remarks.
- Sexualised language, designed to embarrass or cause discomfort.
- Gestures, which are used to depict body parts or sexual intercourse.
- Rumours of a sexual nature about an individual, particularly those that describe sexual behaviour, orientation, deviance, or spreading rumours that imply sexual promiscuity inside or outside the workplace.
- Generalisations about gender, such as alleging that 'all women are neurotic' or 'all women are sluts'.

- Leaving mundane tasks to women, including the washing of cups, purchasing of coffee or biscuits, or maintaining the tidiness of a shared area.
- Being shown pornographic material or having such material on display.
- Unsolicited physical touching that is inappropriate to the relationship with the person who touches or to the context in which it occurs.
- Favouritism towards those who respond to sexual overtures.
- Stalking, both inside and outside the workplace.
- Veiled threats of recriminations if sexual intrusion is not permitted or if sexual favours are not dispensed.
- Veiled promises of rewards if sexual favours are granted.
- Name-calling that has sexual connotations.
- Accusations that promotion or high work status were acquired because of gender or because sexual favours were dispensed.
- Personal questions of an intimate nature to which the questioner has no entitlement to an answer. This may include questions at job interviews about marital status, plans for parenthood or child-minding arrangements.
- Copying or mimicking in an offensive or sexual manner.
- Conducting sexually offensive conversations in the presence of another person.

INDIVIDUAL FACTORS AFFECTING SEXUAL BULLYING

The effects of sexual bullying are many and varied and may depend on the previous life experiences of the person who is exposed to them. For example, a person who has previously been a victim of physical or sexual abuse may experience any form of sexual innuendo or sexual advance as intrusive, abusive or threatening.

The personality of the victim may also play a part in the manner in which a person might perceive or deal with sexual bullying. Those who are more outgoing, more socially skilled and more confident may be able to retort quickly, nip offensive approaches in the bud or communicate effectively their wish not to be exposed to jokes or material of a sexual nature. This may contrast sharply with the response of a more reserved, sensitive or retiring person.

Age is also a factor in how vulnerable a person may be to sexual bullying. People who are young, inexperienced, ignorant of their rights and more stressed by trying to adapt to life are obvious targets. Likewise, people in older age brackets may be targets for those who enjoy causing embarrassment by using phraseology or gestures which are offensive.

Furthermore, the extent to which a person has other supports in life, such as a wife, husband, children, family, leisure interests, work options or other talents, will influence the degree to which they may be targeted for sexual bullying. These supports may also help determine whether the person fights back or becomes helpless, hopeless or depressed by the bullying.

The personality of the perpetrator is also a factor in the conduct of sexual bullying. Inability to handle power, or a personality that seeks and enjoys power and control, may influence a person's tendency to bully others. Those who feel disappointed by their status within a company may take their frustrations out on those in weaker positions. They may also try to establish a sense of importance by wielding power over subordinates.

People who are fearful of losing control over employees and who have not been adequately trained in management may also resort to using primitive and authoritarian controls to maintain authority. Research also shows that those who are intimidated by the competence, ability or assertiveness of other workers, especially if they are female, may respond in a bullying manner. Finally, most sexual bullying is perpetrated by those who suffer deep-seated fears about their own sexual ability, orientation or stability.

SOCIAL FACTORS CONTRIBUTING TO SEXUAL BULLYING

Both men and women are sexually bullied, but 90% of complaints of sexual harassment are made by women. This is because women have traditionally been vulnerable to harassment, not only in society at large but also in the workplace where they hold the majority of low-grade, part-time and lower-paid jobs.

Studies indicate that the prevalence of violence against women is high in Ireland. Statistics published by the Rape Crisis Centre and by women's refuges, together with figures for women seeking barring orders against violent husbands and the reported increases in sexual crime, support the idea that Ireland has inadequately tackled sexual harassment and violence at a social level.

The traditional historical dominance of men in the workplace and at the centre of political, social and economic power, in addition to the hierarchical employment situation where women are located amongst the lower ranks, has created an environment in which women may be sexually discriminated against.

Both UK and Irish research show that victims of bullying are more likely to be bullied by their superiors than by their equals. Given that women account for less than 25% of executive, managerial or administrative positions, they are thus more likely to be targets of sexual bullying.

Men who are sexually bullied have to contend with the

macho images which society constructs for them. Because of these images, men are more likely to feel ashamed, silenced and unwilling to admit that they are being sexually bullied. They may be inhibited from disclosing their experience or from formally making complaints.

Furthermore, some men now complain that they are exposed to double standards. In other words, they say that if they use the mildest of provocative language in the presence of women, this may be construed as sexual harassment. By way of contrast, they say that women do not feel any need to protect men from their expletives.

Society's views of women, including the objectifying and commodifying of women in advertising and pornography, contribute to the message that women are fair-game for sexual innuendo. However, men are increasingly finding themselves the targets of commodification in advertising, thus contributing to the conditions in which they may also be targets for sexual bullying.

THE CONSEQUENCES OF SEXUAL BULLYING
The consequences of sexual bullying are many and far-reaching, affecting the individual who is being sexually bullied, the other employees who are witness to the bullying, the tone and tension levels in the work environment, general organisational effectiveness, levels of absenteeism, staff turnover and, of course, productivity and profits.

Personal consequences
The personal consequences of sexual bullying range from embarrassment, discomfort and upset to psychological distress and post-traumatic stress. The impact on the individual will depend on the severity and the duration of the sexual bullying, the possibility for escape and the resistance

and personality of the person targeted for abuse.

The consequences of sexual bullying may include fear for one's good name, especially if sexual innuendo or rumour is circulated. There are also fears for one's position in a company if the job is likely to be terminated or if resignation is the only option. Fears that one's prospects of promotion will be diminished or frozen are often cited, particularly if it is implied that sexual favours are required in order to advance in a company.

Victims of sexual bullying and innuendo may experience the following:

- Embarrassment, discomfort and distress.
- Anger and feelings of helplessness.
- Fear of sexual inadequacy.
- Poor self-esteem and loss of self-confidence.
- Fear of reprisal if complaints are made.
- Unhappiness in the workplace and daily dread of having to attend.
- Difficulty sleeping as a result of stress.
- Fear of being raped or sexually molested.
- Reduced attendance at work through illness or psychological distress.
- Sense of increasing isolation.
- Feelings of depression.
- Feelings of suspiciousness or paranoia, where every communication becomes suspect.
- Deterioration in ability to work, thereby exacerbating loss of confidence, sense of vulnerability and sense of inadequacy.
- Deterioration in all relationships at work.
- Deterioration in relationships at home, as work stress spills into home environment.

- Deterioration in friendships outside the workplace, especially if friends are overly-subjected to the topic or overburdened by demands for support.
- Fears for sanity.
- Fears for self, for good name and for safety.
- Thoughts of suicide, especially if feeling trapped, disbelieved or unable to retaliate.

Organisational consequences

Certain organisational or managerial styles facilitate sexual bullying. These include exploitative, authoritarian or inflexible leadership, role ambiguity, poorly-defined task structures, blind cohesiveness in group compositions which are intolerant of difference or diversity, significant gender inequalities in employment practices, inadequate conflict management training, lack of specific policies with regard to bullying and sexual harassment, poor information flow to employees about policies, procedures and their rights with regard to bullying and sexual harassment.

Organisations bear many consequences of sexual bullying. High rates of absenteeism, caused by the psychological or physical ill-health of employees, are experienced. Productivity is likely to be reduced substantially. Loyalty to the organisation will be reduced if it is seen to be facilitating sexual bullying. Initiative and creativity are likely to be stifled. There is likely to be a high staff turnover, as those who find themselves without redress seek employment elsewhere.

Some further consequences of sexual bullying in the workplace are as follows:

- Reduced attendance at work because of stress-related illness.

- Decreased performance, concentration, decision-making and consequent poor efficiency and productivity.
- Increased likelihood of accident or injury due to stress-related carelessness.
- Poor staff morale, as dissatisfaction extends to those who witness the bullying.
- Poor teamwork.
- Demotivation, lethargy, apathy and occupational burn-out.
- Fears by other staff members that they may be the next target.
- Increases in industrial action.
- Potential for costly legal suits.

RESOLUTIONS

The problem of sexual bullying can be overcome by the determination of those who are abused to disclose the abuse and to outwit the sexual bully. Changes at organisational level are also required in many workplaces so that a climate of sexual bullying is not tolerated, and should it occur it is dealt with swiftly and effectively.

If you think that you are a victim of sexual bullying, the following suggestions may be useful:

- Do not rush in with wild and unsubstantiated accusations at the first indiscretion. The apparent act of bullying may result from an ill-timed joke, an unfortunate gaffe or an error of judgement without any bullying or malicious intent.
- If in doubt about whether your perception of a possible case of sexual bullying is valid, try to elicit the help or cooperation of another employee of similar status to

you to observe and verify your interpretation of the situation.

- Analyse the communications that have occurred. Make a note of the specific words used and the tone or perceived intent of those words.
- Ensure that you have not contributed to the other person misjudging your communications or wishes.
- If possible, be assertive at the very first sexual innuendo, joke or touch. Clearly and loudly let it be known that you do not wish to hear such remarks or jokes and that you find them offensive. Nipping initial advances in the bud can be very effective and establishes the working boundaries.
- Establish if the situation can be resolved by talking directly to the perpetrator and reaching agreement about acceptable boundaries of behaviour.
- A loud request to a sexual bully to remove their hand from your person, or a loud statement of regret that you cannot supply the sexual favour that has been requested, often works wonders. Remember that all forms of bullying thrive on secrecy, intimidation and shame.
- Be aware of the consequences of making allegations of sexual bullying which are serious and which you cannot substantiate. However, do not let fear deter you from making the appropriate disclosures. It is likely that the sexual bully is known and has a record of bullying.
- Ascertain if there has been a greater than usual staff turnover in the department in which you are working or in other departments working directly with the person who is sexually bullying you.
- If possible, establish contact with others who have been sexually bullied so that complaints are made by a num-

ber of staff.

- Take precise notes of where you and the bully were physically situated during an encounter you regard as bullying.
- Contrive a situation in which the sexual bully may feel safe but will be overheard or interrupted. For example, you may ask a friend or colleague to join you in a room or at some other location in which the bullying is likely to take place.
- If offensive visual material is left on your desk, keep it as evidence.
- Offensive computer material should also be stored as evidence.
- Ensure that anyone you approach for medical or other help keeps records of your visitations and treatments.
- Consult with the personnel department or the relevant staff support officers in your organisation, such as welfare officers, psychologists, counsellors, pastoral care teams or other designated staff supports.
- Establish the proper process and procedures for making a complaint within the company and ensure that all procedures are carried out correctly.
- In extreme cases, where no other redress is forthcoming, personal legal action may need to be considered.

BULLYING AT HOME

Domestic violence is a serious assault on family life. When this form of bullying occurs, it affects all family members whether they be perpetrators, victims, participants or witnesses.

Domestic bullying can range from occasional outbursts of anger to endless, relentless, aggressive assaults on the happiness, the health and the emotional sensibilities of family members. Tragically, it may include the neglect and emotional deprivation of children, physical injury to them, or the ultimate betrayal of childhood through sexual abuse.

Domestic violence and bullying can involve assaults on parents by adolescents and even adult children. It may involve brothers and sisters in combat with each other for parental approval or for affection and attention.

It can take the form of neglect or cruelty to aged, dependent parents. It may involve an assault by wives on the psychological well-being of husbands, attacks on their masculinity and sometimes even physical attacks on their person.

It may involve a complex cycle of conflict between husbands and wives. Indeed, one study shows that at least 16% of couples have one violent interaction annually.

BULLYING IN MARRIAGE
Bullying and violence in marriage may take the form of wife-battering. Indeed, male violence is often cited as one of the primary hazards to health in the home. One study showed that wife-battering accounted for 25% of all violent crime. A further study found that as many as 20% of

women had been assaulted during marriage.

Over 30% of women experienced violence in one disadvantaged Dublin community, and if the thousands of applications made annually to the courts by women for barring orders against their husbands are any measure of bullying, then the problem is very extensive.

Husbands are not immune to bullying by wives. One American study found that almost 5% of women had engaged in aggression towards their husbands. This often takes the form of verbal aggression, throwing objects or breaking objects, and women are reportedly six times more likely to throw objects than men. Studies also show that violent verbal exchanges in the home often escalate into physical violence.

BULLYING OF CHILDREN

Children are particularly vulnerable to bullying at home and this abuse of power is one of the saddest betrayals of trust. Both men and women betray children when they diminish, humiliate, neglect, injure or hurt them.

Research suggests that women are more likely to abuse children, particularly where the women are young parents, have a number of young children with close spacing between them and have experienced being abused themselves as children. Feelings of depression and lack of support exacerbate the problem.

With regard to sexual abuse, some statistics show that 90% of all child sexual abusers are men and as many as 75%–80% are known to the child.

However, statistical reports on abuse vary. For example, one study estimated that one-third of all adults were abused as children. In a further study of 930 women, one-quarter of them had been sexually abused by the time they reached the age of fourteen.

Whatever the variation in statistics, there is no doubt that bullying of children, particularly involving sexual abuse and violence, is of serious dimensions.

CAUSES OF BULLYING

If bullying is the exercise of power by one person over another, then it is not surprising that bullying might take place in the complex web of relationships that constitutes a family.

Living in harmony together requires that people often have to subvert their independence and their wishes to the needs and requirements of others. Having to do so constantly can be a strain. Whenever you have people exercising their own individuality or imposing their wishes on the collective, problems become pronounced. This is how bullying arises.

At the core of domestic bullying lies a large number of possible precipitators, ranging from minor irritants to significant psychological distress. The following are some of the factors which might contribute to bullying in the home:

- The stresses and strains of living in close proximity. In particular, cramped and crowded conditions are more likely to lead to outbursts of frustration, annoyance and anger.
- Having to share scarce resources, food, money or household facilities. Bullying between brothers and sisters often arises for this reason, with the more powerful or cunning dominating the weak.
- Being stressed by financial problems, resulting in anxiety, anger or a sense of powerlessness. This may lead one partner to 'manage the money', a power which can

be both bullying and punitive.

- Holding different views of parenting. This can cause conflict at a very deep level, particularly if one parent regards the other as being either excessively lenient or excessively harsh.
- Holding different views of male and female roles, especially when the traditional male dominant position is challenged and rejected.
- Being a single parent. Practical problems or psychological stress may leave someone who is parenting alone more vulnerable to and less able to cope with unreasonable demands made by their children.
- Having experienced violence and bullying at home as a child. Research suggests that if the experiences of childhood are not addressed, cycles of bullying and victimisation can be perpetuated from one generation to the next.
- Experiencing problems outside the home. It is not unusual for disillusionment and anger arising in the workplace to find expression in the home. This may bring about the classic bullying hierarchy where the boss reprimands a husband, who returns home and hits his wife, who slaps the children who, in turn, tease the pet.
- Undergoing unwanted 'role reversal', where a husband and wife are forced to swap roles. This is not uncommon where there is unexpected male redundancy or unemployment. Having to reverse roles can lead to stresses that may precipitate bullying in either partner.
- Being tired, feeling overworked, feeling unappreciated. Children are often the recipients of anger arising in this way.
- Having a large family, close spacing of children and few supports.

- Dealing with the emotional needs of teenagers. Young people who are experiencing their own difficulties during the teenage years can induce considerable worry, fear, guilt or anger in their parents. The parents may respond by introducing rigid controls that spill over into bullying.
- Coping with alcohol or substance abuse in the family. One study has suggested that up to 80% of wife-battering is brought about by the consumption of alcohol.
- Being alcohol dependent. Alcohol abuse in women is a major factor in child neglect and may result in the emotional and physical abuse of their children.
- Suffering physical illness or disability. The stress of dependence can sometimes lead a person to emotionally bully their carer. Alternatively, looking after chronically-ill or disabled family members can become burdensome to the point where resentment develops into coercive, unresponsive or bullying behaviour towards the dependent person.
- Suffering fears of rejection or fears of abandonment. Research shows that parents with emotional insecurities or immaturities may perceive normal developmental events, such as a baby crying or a toddler having a tantrum, as a rejection by the baby or as a deliberate, provocative action by the child. The response may be aggressive and violent.
- Suffering from feelings of inadequacy or jealousy. These feelings can lead to unfounded suspiciousness, restrictions on the partner's movements, the monitoring of phone calls, questioning, accusing, withholding of money or attempts to force admissions of guilt from the partner.
- Having excessive 'house proud' aspirations. These can

take the form of extreme demands for tidiness, clean-iness, household repairs and decoration and other un-reasonable household demands.

- Experiencing sexual problems. Clinical findings suggest that male impotence, or partial male impotence, can be a major cause of violence towards wives who may be blamed for the problem.
- Female sexual problems may also lead husbands to feel inadequate, rejected or frustrated. Unaddressed sexual problems can translate into bullying behaviour.
- Having unmet childhood needs which are carried into marital relationships. These can include excessive ex-pectations of marriage or seeking total nurturance from the partner in the home. The resulting strains can cause bullying behaviour.

SOCIAL CAUSES OF BULLYING

In addition to the personal and family issues that may cause domestic bullying, a number of other factors in-cluding beliefs, attitudes and practices in society also con-tribute to the prevalence of bullying in the home. The fol-lowing are some examples:

- The legal distinction between violence in the home and violence in public places, perpetuating the belief that one is less serious than the other. Also, the reported dif-fering responses to complaints about assault in both contexts.
- The residue of archaic legal and social beliefs that women are the possessions of husbands and that child-ren are the possessions of parents. For example, the 'rule of thumb' is a term which derives from the mea-sure of the thickness of the object with which one was

permitted to hit one's wife.

- Levels of violence in society and general attitudes to pornography.
- Depictions of gratuitous violence or coercive sexuality on film and video at a level that may desensitise people towards violence or suggest that it is acceptable.
- Allowing bullies to evade responsibility for their behaviour by pleading that they were under the influence of alcohol. Alcohol consumption may be used to excuse unacceptable bullying behaviour.
- Environments of poverty and social deprivation in which adults are unable to cope with their emotions and those of their children.
- Unemployment, with consequent loss of self-esteem. Unemployed men often feel that they are failing in their traditional roles. As a result, they may assert authority in the home to regain a sense of importance. Additionally, any adverse responses from wives may evoke hurt, control and retaliation.
- Participating in an educational system that, in the past, sanctioned corporal punishment. Using punishment rather than dialogue or guidance may be the approach to relationships used by some who were brought up in this system.

Manifestations of bullying

Bullying in the home can manifest itself in many ways, ranging from subtle psychological controls right through to persistent and explosively violent behaviour.

Bullying often involves callous unconcern towards others, a notable lack of empathy for others and an inability to assume another's point of view or to imagine how others must be feeling.

It can involve ruthlessly imposing one's own will, making insincere promises, letting others down or embarrassing others in company.

The following are some of the forms that bullying in the home can take:

- Using family resources for personal enjoyment at the expense of the needs and rights of other family members.

- Cutting off family members from social contacts and leisure outlets. Friends may not be permitted to visit or to be visited.

- Designating where people may go and demanding unreasonable accounts of every movement and social encounter. This is not to be confused with the normal vigilance that parents exercise with regard to children, to ensure their safety.

- Making family members suffer the embarrassment of inadequate, shoddy or out of fashion clothing, particularly at the developmental stages when keeping up with friends is important.

- Restricting food. Measuring and counting what may be eaten or drunk and designating who will be deprived. Using food deprivation as punishment.

- Depriving family members of heat or light. In extreme cases, fuses have been removed from electric fuse boxes. Also, leads of television sets or essential parts of household equipment have been removed so that they cannot be enjoyed in the bully's absence.

- Depriving family members of money, leaving them without independent financial means and dependent on the mood or whim of the bully.

- Making threats of sanctions, punishments and restric-

tions. Using inconsistent discipline, making contra-
dictory demands and using intimidation and fear to
gain advantage or compliance.

- Using physical punishments and physical violence.
Children have been beaten, burnt, tied up, punched,
kicked, bitten, starved, frightened and abused.
- Wife-battering and husband-battering, including the
use of verbal or physical violence.
- Conflict between children. In particular, older children
can be intimidating, emotionally castigating, physically
cruel or even sexually abusive.

EFFECTS ON THE ADULT OF DOMESTIC BULLYING

Bullying in the home is clearly not conducive to a happy
family life. Constant bullying can undermine the confidence, self-esteem, social skills and the feeling of competence of those who are bullied. Serious bullying, which involves physical violence, can be life-threatening for family
members. The many negative consequences for adults who
have been bullied may include the following:

- Becoming withdrawn and afraid to speak about the
bullying.
- Being increasingly absent from work.
- Experiencing problems with concentration, memory,
organisation or with coping.
- Becoming cut off from friends.
- Becoming cut off from extended family.
- Experiencing sleep disturbances.
- Developing stress-related physical illnesses.
- Developing anxiety and depression.
- Experiencing panic attacks or other manifestations of
mental ill-health.

- Turning to alcohol or other substances to reduce the pain.
- Experiencing a feeling of being trapped, increased helplessness and powerlessness.
- Losing trust in others.
- Becoming increasingly fearful for safety.
- Becoming increasingly fearful for the welfare of children at home.
- Feeling suicidal or wishing one was dead.

EFFECTS ON CHILDREN OF DOMESTIC BULLYING

The effects of bullying on children are considerable, but the depth of a child's distress will depend on many factors. These include the level or severity of the bullying, when it began, when it ended and the range and extent of supports and resources available to the child.

Other factors determining the effects on a child include whether the bullying was also inflicted equally on brothers and sisters. Furthermore, if people were available to comfort, praise and reassure the child, then the bullying may have been diluted by the kindness, warmth and affirmation derived from these sources. Likewise, because children frequently blame themselves for the behaviour of adults, if there were explanations available to the child of the real cause of the bullying then the experience of guilt may be avoided.

Other effects on children may include the following:

- Unhappiness, tearfulness, looking sad and upset, expressing sadness or becoming emotionally cut off.
- Frozen facial expressions, fearfulness, with rigid or defensive body postures.
- Withdrawal from adults or flinching in the presence of adults.

- Extremes of behaviour, such as being excessively restless and demanding, seeking attention or being excessively timid and withdrawn.
- Changes in night behaviour, including upset, inability to sleep, fear, night terrors, nightmares.
- Persistent bedwetting for which no medical cause has been found, or soiling.
- Complaints of stomach aches or other physical ailments.
- Regressive behaviour, including thumb-sucking, holding a teddy or reverting to a previous stage.
- Poor school performance, poor concentration, inattention, lack of confidence, fear of speaking out and a reluctance to provide the 'news of the day'.
- Bullying those who are younger and weaker. This is a common response to being bullied at home. Bullying behaviour is most often learned behaviour.
- Hiding, being secretive, running away from home.
- Confusion about how to behave. Studies show that children who are severely physically punished for being aggressive become more aggressive. In this way, a dangerous cycle develops.

EFFECTS OF DOMESTIC BULLYING ON ADOLESCENTS

Because of the different developmental stage of the adolescent, the experiences of being bullied and the expressions of distress will be different from those demonstrated by the child. Adolescents often exhibit some of the following:

- Extreme behaviour and mood swings, expressions of anger and aggression or cynicism about adults, which are out of proportion to the adolescent's stage of development.

- Difficulty sleeping and complaining about a range of physical ailments.
- Developing feelings of depression, including tearfulness, irritability, feelings of powerlessness, helplessness and hopelessness.
- Changes in eating patterns, looking sad and expressing sadness and unhappiness.
- Complaints about difficulty in concentrating.
- Self-loathing and attaching little worth to one's person.
- Abusing substances, such as alcohol or drugs.
- Poorer school performance than would be expected for age or ability.
- Running away from home. This is one of the most common cries for help amongst young people.
- Reckless disregard for safety of self or of others.
- Self-destructive or self-mutilating behaviours.
- Becoming sexually promiscuous, which is particularly common amongst those who have been sexually abused.
- Being tortured by guilt, especially if unable to protect other family members from the bully.
- Modelling or adopting similar bullying behaviour towards others within or outside the family.
- Threatening suicide or attempting suicide.

EASING THE STRAIN

External solutions

Before attempting to tackle bullying in the home, decisions need to be taken about whether or not a couple or a family can end the bullying problem by themselves or whether outside professional, marital, medical, psychiatric or legal intervention is required. In cases of serious physical violence, sexual abuse, persistent bullying or chronic family dysfunction, outside help and intervention may well be essential.

Unfortunately, there are sad and tragic instances where the only solution may be the removal of the bully from the home or the removal of other family members for their safety. These cases normally arise where children cannot be protected or where family members fear for their health, their safety or even their lives.

There are also situations where the bully has been diagnosed with a serious psychiatric disorder and is unable or unwilling to receive help. Again, the protection and safety of other family members is of paramount importance when such a situation arises.

General practitioners are usually aware of the appropriate local services for men, women and children and for families in conflict or suffering the effects of bullying. The headquarters of each Regional Health Board will provide the address of local health centres from whom information on supports can be obtained. Other references are listed at the end of the book.

Internal conflict solutions
When bullying has not progressed to a level requiring professional intervention or the removal of the family to a place of safety, there are many ways that families can address the problem of bullying in their home. The following strategies may be helpful:

- Identify all positive qualities in the family's relationships. Make a note of the family's strengths and affiliations.
- Identify the sources of stress and strain for each family member.

- Examine which of those stresses can be alleviated, which can be cured and which must be endured (for example, financial pressures and work pressures or the pressures of adolescence and old age).
- Make a commitment to resolve the problems. Specify the changes required, by whom they need to be made and how soon they need to occur.
- List supports that might be obtained. For example, consider baby-sitting or help from families or friends. Avoiding loneliness and isolation is particularly important for women who find themselves bullying their children.
- Examine modes of communication and patterns of communication. Often, cycles of negative interaction can be identified and can be resolved by a change in communication style.
- Create time and a place to talk. Family meetings can be useful for decision-making. Issues can be discussed, including holiday plans and the allocation of household tasks, while individual complaints can be addressed.
- Make practical plans to avoid conflict. For example, decide how the choice of television viewing is to be made by family members, how computers are to be shared or how material goods are to be distributed.
- Come to terms with the fact that expressions of anger are not helpful. They do not reduce tension and they have no positive value. In fact, research shows the opposite, namely that verbally violent arguments often escalate into physical confrontations.
- Identify the triggers of anger and violence. Plan how to recognise them. Decisions should be made about what each person must do when such triggers are observed. For example, it might be decided that a wife will leave

the room or that a husband will leave the house for a while.

- Become aware of the physical feelings of anger and learn how to initiate relaxation and anger management strategies. Help children to engage in relaxation techniques. Some parents find the use of aromatherapy, scented candles, incense or relaxing music conducive to creating a relaxed home environment.

- Take a course in assertiveness. In this way, family members may learn how to assert themselves appropriately rather than impose themselves aggressively. Additionally, weaker members may learn how not to be imposed upon.

- Identify the bullying behaviours in the family and list all the benefits that a person obtains through their bullying behaviours. Examine how some of these benefits might be achieved by behaving in a non-bullying manner.

- In the case of children, decide what sanctions will be imposed for the use of bullying tactics.

- Establish rules of acceptable behaviour that apply to all family members. For example, establish that physical hitting is not allowed. Ensure that certain types of verbal exchanges are banned, such as name-calling or denigrating remarks that are hurtful.

- Husbands and wives should provide each other with a sympathetic assessment of their partner's stresses and strains. Putting oneself in the other person's shoes can invoke a greater understanding of what life is like for that person.

- Tackle practical problems. For example, arguments over housework may be resolved by paying someone else to undertake these tasks. Where finances do not allow for this, a fair distribution of household tasks can be worked out, which take account of the age of family members and the other demands being made on them.

- Make sure that your expectations are realistic. Don't treat set-backs as failures. Instead, regard them as obstacles to be overcome or opportunities for new learning.

With the exception of serious bullying, most of the usual stresses and strains that cause conflict in families pass with time. Young children grow up, adolescents mature and become responsible adults and couples learn to live with each other in realistic appreciation of each other's differences. Bullying in the home is not inevitable but is something that can be avoided, addressed, managed and resolved, if necessary with help from outside.

BULLYING IN OLD AGE

Just as the beginning of life is a time of fragility and vulnerability, so too are the closing years a time of frailty and dependence. It is this reliance on others that makes old age a time of susceptibility to bullying and abuse. It is estimated that one in ten elderly persons living with a family member may be subjected to some form of abuse.

Old age is often referred to as the 'second childhood' because of this return to dependence on others for support, physical care, emotional nurturance, psychological attention, safety and protection and even for assistance in the routine activities of daily living.

Old age, therefore, is a time of progressive decline and loss. Sadly, it can also be a time when the unscrupulous, the greedy, the cold and calculating, the unfeeling or the opportunistic may take advantage of an old person.

What is disturbing is the number of elderly people who may become victims of bullying through physical neglect, emotional isolation, financial exploitation, coercion to hand over their resources, intimidation and threat and even physical assault, battering and sexual abuse.

ATTITUDES TO THE ELDERLY

In modern western cultures, the elderly are often perceived as a problem for society, a burden to their relatives, an encumbrance on the state and a drain on medical and social resources. Respect has been replaced by ridicule, deference by indifference, devotion by disdain or by the discrimination of ageism.

Furthermore, social, environmental and medical advances ensure that people live longer than at any other time in history. The biblical reference of 'three score and ten', which represented extraordinary life-span, is now a normal life expectancy. The resulting disproportionate number of elderly people dependent on a relatively smaller population of young people has resulted in the elderly being perceived as an economic burden on society. In this environment, the elderly are more vulnerable to bullying.

Other social changes include the following:

- Changes in family structure. Whereas in the past the family was a unit composed of several generations living close together, today it is more often limited to parents and young children.
- Working parents. Families in which both parents work are not conducive to providing accommodation for elderly family members.
- Separation and divorce. Many elderly people whose children divorce find that they are deprived of contact with their grandchildren. Therefore, young people may have little positive exposure to the elderly or opportunities to develop warm attachments with them.
- Levels of crime and violence in society. Old people have become targets for robbery and violence.
- Emphasis on productivity, consumerism and materialism. This emphasis takes a negative view of the elderly's economic contribution and of their usefulness and value to society.
- Mandatory retirement. This may be interpreted by others either as a welcome reprieve from work or as a message that one is useless and redundant.
- Ageism. Cultures that emphasise youth, attractiveness, success and power may have little time for the elderly.

- Ethical codes. Diminished morality and unethical business practices may lead to exploitation of the elderly.

CHANGES IN OLD AGE

As with all cases of bullying behaviour, whether it be at school, at home or in the workplace, there are certain conditions which facilitate bullying. Changes making for a greater vulnerability in the elderly include the loss of a partner, loss of mental capacity, reduced physical health and strength, accidents or injury, changes in financial circumstances, experiences of grief or depression and changes in emotional disposition through poor adjustment to ageing.

The following are some of the life events, physiological, intellectual and social changes that contribute to progressive dependence, thereby making old people more susceptible to being bullied:

Longer life-span

In the past it was common for wives to die in childbirth or for men to die in middle-age. Now, with longevity, couples may live together for fifty years or more. The potential for marital conflict and divorce is increased.

Furthermore, with longevity, an increasing number of adult children find themselves in caring capacities, often in accommodation that is overcrowded and with lifestyles that do not lend themselves to a caring role. Abuse may result.

Death of a spouse

The loss of a partner and protector can leave a previously active, content person without companionship. The remaining partner may be unable or afraid to live alone.

Men who are unused to cooking or cleaning or women

who are unused to managing financial affairs may be forced to rely on others for help.

Accident or injury

Slower speed and stiffness in the joints can put older people at risk. They may be less adept at judging the speed and proximity of oncoming traffic, thereby exposing themselves to the risk of accident.

A fall in old age will cause shock and worry. Bones are less dense and there is an increased risk of breakage. The subsequent nervousness and dependence can cause a previously independent person to become needy and dependent.

Financial problems

Changes in the cost of living and unexpected pressures on financial resources can cause unforeseen poverty or dependence on family members.

It is not unusual for the elderly to have valuable property but a poor income. The unscrupulous can suggest the sale of property or the signing over of property in return for care. Care may then be denied, inadequately provided, neglectful or even abusive.

Health problems

Many factors may contribute to ill-health, including loneliness, poverty, under-nourishment and unhappiness. There may be greater susceptibility to illness, with minor illnesses causing debilitation.

Old age is also a time of sensory and motor impairment. There may be breathlessness after exertion and reduced strength and speed of movement. The result may be increased vulnerability and dependence.

Reduced mobility

Older people may be unable to drive due to nervousness or anxiety, the cost of maintaining a car or medical problems. Impaired driving skill may also arise from a variety of ageing processes including slower reaction time, slower recovery to an anxious moment, poorer dark vision and reaction to glare, reduced perceptual and motor functions.

Physical mobility is reduced. Arthritis and rheumatism often occur. Help may be required for simple tasks such as shopping and housework and for tasks involving lifting, carrying, bending and manipulating.

Visual deterioration and hearing problems

Loss of visual ability may create a range of dependencies. Being unable to hear properly can cut the person off from conversation and social exchange, cause problems in following instructions adequately or cause irritation in those trying to communicate with the elderly person. Fear of leaving home may result. In some elderly people this fear can develop into panic.

Sleep disturbance

More rest and less sleep are required by the elderly. Sleep patterns are often disturbed, with a return to the sleep pattern of infancy and childhood and more naps being required during the day.

There may be difficulty in falling asleep, waking more often during the night and waking earlier in the morning. There is often a complaint about the quality of sleep.

Studies also conclude that snoring occurs in 60% of men and 40% of women by the time they reach their sixties. The disturbed sleep and snoring patterns of the elderly can cause friction for family members with whom the person is living.

Psychiatric impairment

Rates of suicide and of mental illness rise as age advances. Studies show that one-third of the elderly who are ill have psychiatric problems and 6%-8% of people over the age of 65 suffer from some form of psychosis. It is also estimated that the aged account for 25% of patients in psychiatric hospitals.

Anxiety and depression

Anxiety and depression are understandable reactions to coping with ever-reducing physical capacities, increased health problems, possible financial worries and concerns about the future. It is estimated that 10%–20% of people over the age of 65 suffer from depression.

One of the problems with old age is that depression may not be recognised either by the sufferer or their family. The reason is that the slowing down, the loss of energy, the fatigue, the poor sleep pattern and the changes in appetite that are symptomatic of depression may also be interpreted as the natural reduction of capacities and energy associated with old age.

Bereavement and grief

Old age is a time when one is exposed to loss, particularly the loss of friends and companions. The death of friends who shared similar capabilities, views, history and social status can cause enormous stress and grief.

There is nobody to confide in, to share worries with, to compare symptoms of ageing with, to joke with or to interact with in an equal relationship. Dependence on younger generations therefore increases.

Living alone

Living alone exposes elderly people to risk. They may be overcharged for household repairs or conned into undertaking unnecessary maintenance work on their home or on household appliances. They may be targeted by burglars, receive nuisance phone calls or be exposed to danger when answering the door. As with all the above, their increased vulnerability can lead to dependence and bullying abuse.

Types of bullying

Bullying of old people may take many forms, including neglect, abandonment, theft, extortion, intimidation, physical cruelty or lack of care. The following are some of the sufferings which old people may have to endure:

Physical bullying

Old people require a considerable amount of physical and medical attention as their capacities to help themselves are reduced or eroded with age. Poor care, neglect and bullying may lead to the following:

- Being physically restrained, including being tied to the bed, hands being tied, movements being restricted or being trapped in cot-like beds.
- Being dirty and untidy. Being left in unmade beds or beds with unchanged linen. If incontinent, being left in own urine or faeces.
- Developing bed sores and pressure sores which are left unattended.
- Being forced to wear unlaundered clothes which are food-stained or dirty.
- Being cold and miserable. Older people react less quickly and less adequately to cold than younger people.

The shivering reflex is poorer and there is the risk of a serious fall in body temperature. Hypothermia, or persistently low body temperature, is a risk for older people who are deprived of adequate heat.

- Being left without new clothes or personal possessions.
- Experiencing malnutrition or suffering from general hunger or thirst. Having to depend on others for every meal and for each drink of water.
- Being given food that is not liked, with no choice of diet or accommodation of individual preference.
- Having to call repeatedly for help. The voice tends to be more restricted in range and in power in old age. Having calls ignored can be distressing and abusive.
- Rough handling when being assisted into or out of bed. This may cause bruising, sprains or the breaking of fragile bones.
- Being deprived of sufficient assistance when walking. This can cause unnecessary falls and injury.
- Being left to suffer with minor ailments. These may include cuts, sore gums, corns and calluses, dry or itchy skin, uncut fingernails.
- Being kept waiting for goods that relatives have been asked to purchase, such as sweets, cigarettes or toiletries. Not knowing how long the wait or deprivation may last.
- Being given excessive medication to induce sleep, silence or immobility.
- Being physically hurt or punished, being shouted at or physically abused.
- Being left without medical care. Having illness neglected and essentially being allowed to fall into ill-health and die.

SOCIAL BULLYING

Elderly people who live with relatives may find they are cut off from previous social contacts and may be excluded and isolated in the relatives' home. This, in itself, is a distressing form of bullying and may include the following:

- Being denied contact with previous neighbourhood or community.
- Being denied access to friends and companions who are not welcomed into the relatives' home.
- Being refused lifts to attend social outings.
- Being denied entertainment, including not being brought to previously enjoyed activities such as bridge, bingo or musical events.
- Being denied access to the family television or being refused a say in the choice of programmes.
- Being confined to a bedroom and not given the freedom of the house.
- Being excluded from family meals, isolated from guests who call to the house or denied the opportunity to join in parties or celebrations.
- Being denied the run of the house, including not being permitted to fix a snack or meal at any time.
- Being cut off from attending religious ceremonies and having priests, ministers or rabbis prevented from visiting the house.
- Being denied an independent means of existence by placing controls on personal finances.
- Being left in the care of an unsuitable or uncaring minder.
- Being put out of the family home, sent to a nursing home and abandoned without further visits or contact.

Psychological bullying

While a lot of old age bullying may be physical or socially isolating, other forms of bullying are psychological and cause enormous pain and hurt. The following are some ways in which an old person may be psychologically bullied:

- Being ignored, disregarded, derided or having opinions dismissed as old-fashioned.
- Having worries dismissed or ignored.
- Having decisions made by others without any consultation.
- Having nobody to talk to or to express sadness or unhappiness to.
- Never receiving a hug, a smile, a caress or any touch that indicates love or concern.
- Being treated with disdain, being talked about as if not present.
- Being shouted at and insulted.
- Being warned, intimidated or threatened with physical abuse.

The effects of being bullied

The effects of being bullied pervade every aspect of an old person's life including their physical health, their social contacts and their emotional and psychological well-being. They may include the following:

- A sense of betrayal, hurt and sadness that at the end of life so much disregard could be shown. This sense of betrayal is particularly acute if the bullies are family members from whom the old person would have expected care and protection.
- Feelings of obsolescence, redundancy and of serving

no useful function. It is not uncommon for the elderly to refer to themselves in derogatory terms such as 'useless', 'on the scrap heap' or 'past their sell-by date'.

- Loss of dignity and loss of self-respect. This is felt particularly by those who are immobile, who are incontinent and who are dependent on others to maintain their personal cleanliness.
- Learned helplessness, which is the belief that you have no control over your life and that it is in the control of others.
- Loss of self-esteem and loss of belief in personal worth or value.
- Feelings of loneliness and being unloved and unlovable.
- Feelings of abandonment, especially if put into a nursing home.
- Upset at loss of assets and finances, which may have been commandeered by relatives.
- Fears and phobias, including the fear of leaving home (agoraphobia) because of the threat and danger in the outside world.
- Shame at the treatment by relatives and a reluctance to disclose what is happening out of family loyalty.
- Despair, depression, feelings of misery, helplessness and hopelessness.
- Suicidal thoughts or the act of suicide itself.

SOME OTHER EFFECTS

Bullying of the aged can arise inadvertently out of the anger, frustration or helplessness of carers. However, a number of common, serious abuses may arise due to the calculated designs of carers, relatives or those empowered to look after the old person. Many of these relate to finances or family possessions and include the following:

- Theft, ranging from money taken from the old person's purse or home to jewellery and valuables stolen from a sufferer of dementia.
- Pension money being withheld, once the pension book is signed over to a relative for collection.
- Social welfare abuses, including claims made on behalf of the elderly person who does not receive the benefits. This may also involve making claims for providing care although the old person is denied that care.
- Fraud, such as tricking an elderly person into handing over shares, assets or property. This may also involve forcing the person to make a will in favour of the bully, either through subterfuge or threat.
- Intimidation and harassment, including forcing old people to pay protection money in return for their safety or freedom from physical abuse.
- Forcing the victim to hand over power of attorney to those who abuse this function. This abuse may be perpetrated by unscrupulous professionals or by family.
- Withholding of medicines, neglect or murder, with the intention of prematurely claiming an inheritance.

ADVICE FOR OLD PEOPLE

While no one likes to contemplate the possibility of their children, relatives, friends or advisors cheating or ill-treating them in old age, there are many situations in which this can happen.

Daughters may resent having to care for a parent, especially if they have just become free of minding young children. Daughters-in-law may feel burdened if asked to care for a mother-in-law and may ill-treat out of indifference, inability, irritability or anger. Sons or sons-in-law may identify an opportunity to secure scarce finance for their business.

Children may take revenge on their parents or retaliate for real or imagined hurts in childhood. Relatives may not have the emotional or psychological resources necessary to be just and kind.

It is wise, therefore, to make arrangements for every eventuality that might occur in old age. Remember that dementia afflicts one in twenty old people and this proportion increases with advancing years. As a result, the time to make provision for the future is when your mental faculties are intact. The following are some suggestions:

- Ensure that you make solid, reliable, index-linked financial provisions and investments. Take advice from trusted and reputable professionals or institutions.
- Take legal advice about your rights in the event of becoming enfeebled, psychiatrically ill, disabled or mentally incapacitated.
- Make a decision as to who you would trust with power of attorney if you were unable to manage your financial affairs. It is better if this is decided in advance and not imposed on you at a time of incapacity.
- Provide yourself with a hands-free phone, a mobile phone, an alarm system and panic button, implements to aid lifting, opening and to assist mobility.
- Buy an adjustable bed, microwave oven for quick meals, remote controls for television and music systems and an intercom system or video system for the front door. These will be useful immediately and will be available in later years.
- Make your home as user-friendly as possible so that the

minimum of maintenance will be required. Ensure that switches, lights, plugs and appliances are positioned for easy accessibility and use.

- Consider special housing for the elderly. These complexes provide secure living, with catering, laundry and nursing care provided when required. Some elderly people like to buy and settle in while still active and establish a network of friends for the future.

- Visit nursing homes and check out prices and facilities. Make inquiries and get a feel for what it might be like to become a resident. In this way, the choice of location is based on your wishes and not on the wishes or requirements of others.

- Make a will and consider stipulating that it may not be altered without the knowledge of, or without being changed in the presence of, specified, trusted people. In this way, you cannot be easily coerced into making a change.

- If family are moving in with you, lay down ground rules in advance. For example, specify that you will not be left as an unpaid baby-minder or child-minder, that you will retain appropriate privacy and independence and that your friends will continue to have access to your home.

- Think very carefully before selling your home and moving in with other people. If you must sell, it may be better to invest the money and provide for independent care.

FURTHER INFORMATION

The purpose of this closing chapter is to identify sources of help for anyone who is being bullied or who wishes to stop bullying.

If you require help you should contact your doctor or your local health centre or health board. They can deal with your problem directly or refer you to the appropriate services in your area.

For information on local support groups it may be useful to check with your community centre, health centre, citizen's information centre, or check the notice-boards at your parish church, your local library or at your doctor's office.

Community welfare officers and public health nurses throughout the country also provide information on local services and referral procedures.

For emergency service numbers, consult the front pages of your local telephone directory.

Many of the agencies which are listed in this chapter will deal with your problem directly or refer you to an appropriate treatment centre, counselling centre, voluntary organisation or support organisation.

Many agencies have branches in towns and cities throughout Ireland and some of these are listed below. Other addresses and telephone numbers are available from the head office of the relevant organisation.

BULLYING AT SCHOOL

The Anti-Bullying Research and Resource Centre, Trinity College, Dublin. Phone: 01–6772941.

Sticks and Stones Theatre Company, 19 Watkins Square, Dublin 8. Phone: 01–2807065.

Psychological Services, Department of Education and Science, Marlborough Street, Dublin 1. Phone: 01– 8734700. Branches of the psychological services are located in the following parts of the country:

Model School, O'Connell Avenue, Limerick. Phone: 061–315966.

Irish Life Building, 1a South Mall, Cork. Phone: 021–906011.

Raheen Road, Clonmel, Co. Tipperary. Phone: 052–25833.

New Government Buildings, Anne Street, Wexford. Phone: 053–24812.

Office of the Inspectorate, Bridge Street, Sligo. Phone: 071–43219.

Office of the Inspectorate, 3rd Floor, Ross House, Merchant Road, Galway. Phone: 091–500009.

Portlaoise Road, Tullamore, Co. Offaly. Phone: 0506–21363.

BULLYING IN THE WORKPLACE

The Anti-Bullying Research and Resource Centre, Trinity College, Dublin. Phone: 01–6772941.

The Labour Court, Tom Johnson House, Haddington Road, Dublin 4. Phone: 01–6608444.

The Labour Relations Commission (and Rights Commissioners Service), Tom Johnson House, Haddington Road, Dublin 4. Phone: 01–6609662.

The Health and Safety Authority, 10 Hogan Place, Dublin 2. Phone: 01–6620400.

Employment Equality Agency, 36 Upper Mount Street, Dublin 2. Phone: 01–6624577.

Legal Aid Board, Head Office Administration, St Stephen's Green House, Dublin 2. Phone: 01–6615811.

CHILD AND PARENT

If your child has become distressed or depressed by being bullied or is bullying other children, there are numerous child guidance services throughout the country and many others are being developed nationwide. For up-to-date information contact your local health board.

The following organisations may also be able to help:

Childline. Freephone 1800 666 666.

Parentline (Organisation for Parents under Stress), Carmichael House, North Brunswick Street, Dublin 7. Phone: 01–8733500.

St Joseph's Adolescent and Family Services, 193 Richmond Road, Fairview, Dublin 3. Phone: 01–8370802.

Mater Dei Counselling Centre, Clonliffe Road, Dublin 3. Phone: 01–8371892.

Barnardo's, Christchurch Square, Dublin 8. Phone: 01–4530355. Barnardo's can also be contacted in Cork. Phone: 021–552100.

CARI (Children at Risk in Ireland Foundation), 110 Lower Drumcondra Road, Dublin 9. Phone: 01–8308529. Also located at Limerick: 2 Garryowen Road, John Street, Limerick. Phone: 061–413331.

In addition to the services for children listed above, there are nationwide branches of the Irish Society for the Prevention of Cruelty to Children. The following are the telephone numbers for these branches:

Limerick. Phone: 061–400077.
Dublin. Phone: 01–6794944.
Galway. Phone: 091–562229.
Kilkenny. Phone: 056–21685.
Wexford. Phone: 053–23864.
Roscommon. Phone: 079–63199.
Drogheda. Phone: 041–33406.
Mullingar. Phone: 044–41744.
Arklow. Phone: 0402–31419.
Monaghan. Phone: 047–84420.
Kildare. Phone: 045–436119.
Louth. Phone: 042–26500.

FAMILY BULLYING

There are many family centres and practising therapists available throughout the country. A list may be obtained from local health boards, health centres and from the Family Therapy Association. A few are listed as follows:

Family Therapy Association of Ireland (FTAI), 17 Dame Court, Dublin 2. Phone: 01–6794055.

The Family Therapy Department, St Vincent's Psychiatric Hospital, Richmond Road, Fairview, Dublin 3. Phone: 01–8370802/8370448.

The Family Therapy Department, Mater Child and Family Services, North Circular Road, Dublin 1. Phone: 01–8034793.

The Family and Marital Therapy Unit, Strand House, 3 Philipsbrough Avenue, Fairview, Dublin 3. Phone: 01–8369900.

Family Mediation Service, Fifth Floor, Block 1, Irish Life Centre, Lr Abbey Street, Dublin 1. Phone: 01–8728277. Also located at 1st Floor, Mill House, Henry Street, Limerick. Phone: 061–312232.

The Clanwilliam Institute, 18 Clanwilliam Terrace, Dublin 2.
Phone: 01–6761363/6762881.

WOMEN AND MEN

Bray Women's Refuge, Heatherwood, Bray, Co. Wicklow.
Phone: 01–2866163 (24 hour helpline).

Women's Refuge, Rathmines, Dublin 6. Phone: 01–4961002.

Adapt House, Women's Refuge Centre, Rosbrien, Limerick.
Phone: 061–412354.

Adapt, Kerry Women's Refuge, Kileen Road, Tralee. Phone:
066–29100.

Women's Aid, Dublin. Freephone 1800 341 900.

Women's Aid, Limerick. Phone: 061–412354.

Women's Aid, Dundalk. Phone: 042–33244.

Rape Crisis Centre. Freephone 1800 778 8888.

70 Lower Leeson Street, Dublin 2. Phone: 01–6614911.

17 Upper Mallow Street, Limerick. Phone: 061–311511.

3 St Augustine Street, Galway. Phone: 091–64983.

(There are also independent centres in the following areas
and help may be sought from these: Athlone, Belfast, Clonmel, Dundalk, Cork, Donegal, Kilkenny, Carlow, Limerick,
Mayo, Tralee, Tullamore, Waterford and Wexford.)

AMEN, 10 St Patrick's Terrace, Navan, Co. Meath. Phone: 046–
23718. Confidential advice line for men in violent relationships.

OLD AGE

Age Action, 114 Pearse Street, Dublin 2. Phone: 01–6779892.
Also located at 30 Camden Street, Dublin 2. Phone: 01–
4785060.

Age and Opportunity, Marino Institute of Education, Griffith

Avenue, Dublin 9. Phone: 01–8370570.

ALONE, 1 Willie Bermingham Place, Kilmainham Lane, Dublin 8. Phone: 01–6791032.

Alzheimer Society of Ireland, St John of God Hospital, Stillorgan, Co. Dublin. Phone: 01–2881282.

The Carers Association. The following are contact addresses and telephone numbers for the association's main centres throughout the country:

St Mary's Community Centre, Richmond Hill, Rathmines, Dublin 6. Freephone 1800 24 07 24. Phone: 01–4974498.

Kellyville Court, 1 Abbeyleix Road, Portlaoise. Phone: 0502–61112.

35 O'Connell Street, Waterford. Phone: 051–857970.

22 Denny Street, Tralee. Phone: 066–21399.

O'Connor Square, Tullamore, Co. Offaly. Phone: 0506–22920.

Psychiatry of Old Age Service (Northside), 16 Eccles Street, Dublin 7. Phone: 01–8600488.

Psychiatry of Old Age Service (Southside), Baggot Street Community Hospital, Baggot Street, Dublin 4. Phone: 01–6681362.

DEPRESSION AND SUICIDE

The Mental Health Association of Ireland, Mensana House, 6 Adelaide Street, Dun Laoghaire, Co. Dublin. Phone: 01–2841166.

AWARE-Helpline, 147 Phibsboro Road, Dublin 4. Phone: 01–6791711.

GROW, National Office, 11 Liberty Street, Cork. Phone: 021–277520. There are other GROW offices at the following locations:

167 Capel Street, Dublin 1. Phone: 01–8734029.

The Ormond Home, Barrack Street, Kilkenny. Phone: 056–61624.

Canada Street, Waterford. Phone: 051–57593.

The Health Centre, Bury Quay, Tullamore. Phone: 0506–51284.

St Loman's Hospital, Mullingar. Phone: 044–40190.

27 Mallow Street, Limerick. Phone: 061–318813.

Tucker Street, Castlebar, Co. Mayo. Phone: 094–26417.

The Samaritans Helpline Callsave 1–850 609 090. The Samaritans can also be contacted as follows:

Dublin. Phone: 01–8277700.

Cork. Phone: 021–271323.

Athlone. Phone: 0902–73133.

Galway. Phone: 091–561222.

Waterford. Phone: 051–872114.

Sligo. Phone: 071–42011.

OTHER SOURCES OF HELP

There are two further sources of help and information which may be very useful in choosing an appropriate and properly qualified therapist. These are as follows:

The Psychological Society of Ireland, 13 Adelaide Road, Dublin 2. Phone: 01–4783913.

(The Psychological Society of Ireland provides an annual list of registered psychologists who have satisfied the society that they have proper qualifications and competence.)

Irish Council for Psychotherapy, 17 Dame Court, Dublin 2. Phone: 01–6794055.

(The Irish Council for Psychotherapy provides a worthwhile publication called *A Guide to Psychotherapy in Ireland*, which includes a list of members and a description of the various approaches to psychotherapy.)

Whatever form bullying takes, there are numerous organisations in this country which provide valuable support and information. It is important to use these resources. It is also important to remember that if you are being bullied or bullying, help is available and the problem can be positively challenged and hopefully resolved.

DEATH AND DYING

Edited by
COLM KEANE

Death and Dying examines responses to bereavement, grief and mourning. Drawing on Irish experts, the book explores normal and abnormal reactions to the death of a spouse, parent, child or loved one. The sensitive issues of suicide, violent death and death by choice are also examined.

The book is presented in an accessible style and is aimed at the general reader. It offers a simple guide on how to cope with bereavement as well as practical advice on where to go for help. The contributors – some of Ireland's most eminent bereavement experts – include psychologists, psychiatrists and medical specialists.

THE SPIRIT OF
TONY DE MELLO

A HANDBOOK OF MEDITATION EXERCISES

JOHN CALLANAN, SJ

This book captures the essence and spirit of Tony de Mello. He was a great teacher. Some said he was a dangerous one. He constantly challenged himself, the world within which he lived and those he came into contact with. For some, this element of challenge was both unsettling and confusing. Tony said that our security does not lie in thoughts or ideas – no matter how profound. Neither does it lie in traditions – no mattered how hallowed. Security can only reside in an attitude of mind and a readiness to reflect deeply, thus subjecting every belief to rigorous questioning.

So, Tony urged people to question, question, question. Questions often make us uncomfortable. They do, however, force us to reflect and thus ensure our growth.

MORE INTERESTING BOOKS

THE TEENAGE YEARS

MARIE MURRAY & COLM KEANE

The Teenage Years is a guidebook for parents of teenagers. It is written in an easy-to-read and accessible style, and will help Irish parents understand the problems and the difficulties experienced by adolescents.

The authors examine the many problems of growing up including sexuality, friendships, bullying and shyness. The ways in which young people handle everyday problems, stressful events and family tragedies are explored, including bereavement, depression, family separation, drug addiction, alcohol abuse, eating problems, emotional breakdown and the role of discipline. Advice is also given on how to cope with study and examination pressure.

The book is aimed at the non-expert, and provides an invaluable insight into the complicated process of growing up.

NERVOUS BREAKDOWN

Edited by
COLM KEANE

Most Irish families have at one time or another been affected by the bewildering consequences of 'nervous breakdown'. The symptoms and manifestations include depression, panic attacks, addictions, phobias, obsessions, sexual problems and difficulties eating and sleeping. These may result from anxiety, stress, trauma, family pressures, or from events such as job loss or bereavement. If you or your family have experienced any of these problems then this book will be of interest to you.

The book is prepared in an 'easy to read' style and is aimed at the non-expert. It offers simple advice on how to cope with the pressures and stresses of everyday life and it gives practical advice on the treatments available.

Contributors include some of Ireland's most eminent psychologists, psychiatrists and therapists.

THE COURSE OF IRISH HISTORY

EDITED BY T. W. MOODY AND F. X. MARTIN

Though many specialist books on Irish history have appeared in the past fifty years, there have been few general works broadly narrating and interpreting the course of Irish history as a whole, in the light of new research. That is what this book sets out to do; and it is a measure of its success that it is still in demand.

The first of its kind in its field, the book provides a short survey, with geographical introduction, of the whole course of Ireland's history. Based on the series of television programmes first transmitted by Radio Telefis Éireann from January to June 1966, it is designed to be both popular and authoritative, concise but comprehensive, highly selective but balanced and fair-minded, critical but constructive and sympathetic. A distinctive feature is its wealth of illustrations.

The present edition is a revised and enlarged version of the original book. New material has been added, bringing the narrative to the IRA ceasefire of 31 August 1994; the bibliography, chronology and index have been augmented accordingly.